THE ART
of
BOWING
PRACTICE

THE ART
OF
BOWING PRACTICE

The Expressive Bow Technique

by

ROBERT GERLE

Stainer & Bell, London

© 1991 Robert Gerle
First Published in Great Britain by
Stainer & Bell Ltd, 23 Gruneisen Road, London N3 1DZ
Reprinted 2001

British Library Cataloguing in Publication Data
Gerle, Robert
    The art of bowing practice: the expressive bow technique
    1. String instruments. Playing. Techniques
    I. Title
    784.19369143

    ISBN 0-85249-791-1

Printed in Great Britain by Caligraving Limited, Thetford, Norfolk

Photograph by Christian Steiner. Used with permission.

Robert Gerle

Robert Gerle began to study in the Liszt Academy in Budapest at an early age in the class of Geza de Kresz, who was himself a pupil of Hubay, Sevcik and Ysaÿe and a close friend of Flesch, Thibaud and Enesco. He has therefore a thoroughbred technical 'pedigree'.

As a performer, he first won international recognition as a prizewinner in the Thibaud and Geneva Competitions immediately after the Second World War and began the first of many major concert tours in Europe, including solo appearances with the Berlin Philharmonic and the London Royal Philharmonic.

In the 1950s, Robert Gerle was invited by Paul Rolland to the University of Illinois, where he worked with Georges Enesco. He remained closely associated with Rolland, playing for part of the latter's famous film series on violin technique now widely used both in America and England.

This book—which complements his earlier book, *The Art of Practising the Violin* (Stainer & Bell, London, 1983)—comes from long experience as a teacher in many notable American conservatoires (including Manhattan, Peabody and Mannes) and universities such as Southern California, Oklahoma and Ohio. On retiring as Professor of Music and Head of the Instrumental Program in the University of Maryland, at Baltimore (UMBC), he was appointed Adjunct Professor of Music at the Catholic University in Washington, DC.

Combining his teaching with playing and conducting, Robert Gerle includes in his recorded repertoire concertos by Barber, Berg, Delius, Hindemith and Kurt Weill as well as classics such as the Beethoven sonatas (with his wife, Marilyn Neeley), the six sonatas for violin and keyboard by J. S. Bach, the complete Brahms-Joachim Hungarian Dances and the second Vieuxtemps concerto. His conducting engagements regularly take him to Canada and South America as well as guest dates in the United States. The convictions expressed in this book show him to be truly one of America's outstanding string teachers.

CONTENTS

To my teachers and fellow students
at the old Franz Liszt Academy of Music
for their friendship, challenge and inspiration

INTRODUCTION

'L'Archet, c'est Moi!'
(With apologies to Louis XIV)

In the preface to *The Art of Practising the Violin*, I wrote: '...it is the bow technique which will largely determine the artistic category of a player'. Commenting in his review for *Strad* magazine, Mr. Louis Carus expressed the wish that 'this statement could perhaps have been reinforced with a broader analysis of right arm problems'. Since a deeper exploration of bow technique as such was not within the scope of my previous work, I am happy to take up this challenge in the present volume.

The importance of bow technique in string playing cannot be overestimated. After all, it is the *bow* which makes the instrument *sound* and transforms mere symbols on paper into music. From the moment the bow touches the string, it characterizes the sound by its manner of moving, endows it with expression and conveys interpretation as the performer's individual contribution in representing the composer's ideas.

At the same time, it is the bow technique, and particularly its expressive aspect, which tends to be most neglected in the training of string players and least developed in their performance.

More than two centuries ago Leopold Mozart wrote:

> The bowing gives life to the notes...it produces now a modest, now an impertinent, now a serious or playful tone; now coaxing, or grave and sublime; now a sad or merry melody; and is therefore the medium by the reasonable use of which we are able to rouse in the hearers the aforesaid emotions.
>
> *A Treatise on the Fundamental Principles of Violin Playing*
> (Oxford University Press, New York, 1951)

Lucien Capet put it this way:

> The virtuosity of the left hand, even if developed as far as possible, will always carry the stamp of a certain artistic sterility, whereas the bow, by its multiple faculties, will give everyone the possibility of translating the most subtle and profound elements in the interpretations of the Art.
>
> *La Technique Superieure de l'Archèt*
> (Maurice Senart & Cie., Paris, 1916)

As to its neglect, Carl Flesch comments:

> While the level of left-hand technique has reached a much higher point of development than in former days, particularly as to precision, intonational

purity, and as influenced by more rational present-day methods of study, the same cannot be claimed for tonal accomplishment, which has rather retrogressed. The primary cause for this is the fact that the more searching pursuits for mastery of finger technique have automatically relegated the tonal element to second place.

Commenting further on the lack of bow technique:

...the differentiating nuance (shading) has given way to a tempered, lukewarm, watery uniformity, minus all characteristic shadings.

The problems of tone production in Violin Playing
(Carl Fischer, New York, 1934)

Emil Kross laments:

It is deplorable to see so many virtuosi misunderstanding the real object of the violin, —it being a melodic instrument by nature—and instead of working towards this end, to notice their one-sided endeavour to shine through mere technique.

The Art of Bowing
(Carl Fischer, New York, 1897)

These statements can be made today with equal validity, especially for the average player, who remains average largely because of the lack of superior bow technique. Without minimizing the obvious importance of an accurate left-hand technique for pure intonation and expressive vibrato, it is still the player's bow technique which reveals his personality, his uniqueness as a person and artist, and his ability to understand and identify with the composer, expressing the essence and meaning of the music in performance.

In earlier days one needed to hear only a few notes from a Kreisler, Elman or Heifetz to recognize the artist instantly, sight unseen, thanks largely to their uniquely individual and infinitely varied bow technique, proving the truth of the saying, "the Bow is the Soul of the Violin".

Today such a stamp of personality is rare even among the foremost artists. The majority of players are seemingly satisfied with a rather elementary bow technique—unaware of any means to improve it or ignoring the necessity of diligent practice to perfect it—moving the bow back and forth between the frog and tip mechanically, with very little expression, articulation or colour.

There can be many reasons (if no excuses) for this state of affairs. A well-developed bow technique is a much more complex art than that of the left hand. Its goals and problems are more subtle, its progress slower and harder to measure and the solutions to its problems more elusive. The right shape of a phrase, a seamless bow-change, a characteristic accent, sensitive timing, a well-planned crescendo or an eloquent sforzato are the result of countless experiments based on mostly subjective judgments, but leading to, and carried out by, objective technical means. It requires imagination to evoke the 'ideal' sound in one's mind and great persistence in its pursuit, without which the 'ideal' performance cannot be approached, much less attained.

The left-hand technique is more concrete and mechanical. Its progress is more readily apparent and directly measurable, and consequently easier to practise. Because of this, the greatest part of practice time is commonly devoted to left-hand related work. Such disproportionate attention results in a simplistic, insensitive and inadequate bow technique, which, at worst, produces a bland and dull tone, wrong accents, unplanned and unwanted diminuendos and crescendos, unmusical and heavy-handed phrasing, unstylistic and tasteless performances. The French saying, 'Bad taste leads to crime' is certainly true in music.

Today we demand instant progress and solutions. The pressure of contemporary life—coupled with the usual late start of string studies and the consequent lack of thorough musical training—is inimical to the in-depth study of the literature and to the development of a correspondingly advanced bow technique.

Those who '…endeavour to shine through mere technique' misunderstand the meaning of the word and aim for only a very limited aspect of it. For what is 'technique' if not the ability to perform a musical composition *in its totality*, including not only its mechanical framework, but also, and specifically, its expressive and transcendental aspects? A 'good technique' does not mean only the ability to play loud and fast. It must include expression and interpretation, as integral and essential parts of any musical composition, which also have their own 'technique', even if neglected.

The purpose of this book is to point the way to a more expressive bow technique, and to the more meaningful, varied and individual interpretations that such a technique can accomplish.

As a starting point, and as the foundation of an advanced technique, the basic principles of bow technique (often taken too much for granted) are reviewed together with their practical and musical applications. The various indications, explicit in our musical notation system, or inherent in the music itself, are then identified and explored, and the matching bow technique with which to express them is described. Finally, to the extent that they demand technical solutions, articulation and phrasing are discussed and illustrated, as well as clues, which point to a certain interpretational approach among the several possibilities, and their impact on the selection of specific means of bow technique.

Based on this information, players will be able to enlarge their musical vocabulary, to enrich the variety of musical expression and interpretation, and to enhance their technical proficiency in the realization of musical ideas, if only by being invited and challenged to think more deeply about them.

There are no 'only' or 'right' ways in musical interpretation: the final, informed choice must remain the player's, just as the manifestation of his or her artistic personality remains an individual responsibility.

I hope that this book may serve as a useful road-map, pointing out the ways toward the player's chosen goal and ideal, and that it may enable him or her to avoid the many detours, blind alleys and pitfalls lurking on the way.

For this journey, I wish my readers 'bon voyage'.

ACKNOWLEDGMENTS

I am grateful to the following for permission to quote from copyright material:

Carl Fischer Inc.
Carl Flesch, *The Problems of Tone Production in Violin Playing* (New York, 1934)

Carl Fischer Inc.
Emil Kross, *The Art of Bowing* (New York, 1897)

Harcourt Brace Jovanovich Inc.
Roger Sessions, *Harmonic Practice* (New York, 1951). Copyright 1951 and renewed 1979 by Roger Sessions.

Oxford University Press:
Leopold Mozart, *A Treatise on the Fundamental Principles of Violin Playing*, translated by Editha Knocker (New York, 1951)

Every effort has been made to trace owners of copyright material and if anyone has been inadvertently overlooked this will of course be put right in any reprint. My thanks are also due to Cathy Tully for the use of her excellent photographs.

Baltimore, 1990   Robert Gerle

PART ONE

BASIC
BOW TECHNIQUE

DEFINITIONS

WEIGHT	Amount of heaviness; the force which gravity exerts upon a body.
PRESSURE	The exertion of steady weight or force upon a surface by an object in contact with it.
LEVERAGE	The mechanical advantage or power gained by using a lever.
LEVER	A rigid bar or rod that turns on a fixed fulcrum.
FULCRUM	The support on which the lever turns.
POWER	Strength or force capable of being exerted; physical strength.
FORCE	Strength or power exerted upon an object.
TORQUE	The tendency of a force to produce rotation about an axis.
GRAVITY	Heaviness or weight; the force of attraction by which terrestrial bodies tend to fall toward the centre of the earth.
PRONATION	Inward rotation, counter-clockwise (positive pressure).
SUPINATION	Outward rotation, clockwise (negative pressure).
LOCATION	Distance of the bow from the bridge.
AGOGIC ACCENT	Stressing a note by delaying it or holding it beyond its full value.

1 THE BOW AND THE BOW-ARM

There are few human endeavours more complicated, sensitive and delicate than that of drawing a pleasing sound from a stringed instrument. A superior bow technique, no matter how easy and natural the artist may make it appear, is the result of an untold number of contrasting, yet complementary motions and their combinations.

It is the sum total of a constantly changing balance of forces, a sensitive and delicate adjustment of bow-speed and pressure, of constant alternations of tension and release between the muscles and the bow. It is the blending of countless physical, physiological and acoustical properties of the instrument and instrumentalist with the laws of nature, the perfect union between the mechanics of the bow and the actions of the player in the service of musical expression in performance.

To acquire the proficiency needed to make the bow ready and willing to convey our musical intentions, considerable practice time has to be devoted to working on bow technique in general, and on its musical and expressive capabilities in particular. This is what so many young musicians fail to do, hoping that mere repetition will miraculously bring about the desired effect.

While there are more than one legitimate and successful approaches to the art of bowing, as represented by several different 'schools', certain mechanical, physical, physiological and acoustical rules are constant and beyond dispute. These rules, dictated by the nature of player and instrument, must be understood and learned at the outset: they are the key not only to correct playing, but also to continued progress. The application of these rules might vary somewhat according to the player's predilections and his or her individual physical and artistic make-up, but these variations must be the logical outgrowth of, and consistent with, the basic principles.

Bow technique is the combination of two units: the mechanics of the bow and the actions of the bow-arm. These two units are co-ordinated with, and applied to, another two-unit entity: the violin and the left arm. Together they form the mechanism of violin playing.

The bow itself is a more complicated implement than appears at first glance. Although consisting basically of a slightly curved stick of wood and a bunch of horsehair which can be tightened or loosened, the combined properties of these two parts create a number of complications and necessitate various interactions between the bow, the bow-arm and the violin:

(1)   The thickness, elasticity and proportionate weight-distribution of the stick changes constantly between the frog and the tip, and these characteristics themselves vary according to the various bow-makers and their every individual bow.

(2)   The distance between the curved stick and the tightened hairs is different at each point from frog to tip, greatest at the ends and diminishing toward the middle.

(3)   The rate of tension between the stick and the hairs also varies in keeping with the changing distance and resilience of the stick: tauter at the ends, slacker in the middle, similar to a clothes-line.

(4)   The tightening of the bow-hair is influenced by the strength of the particular bow-stick and the player's own preference and bow technique. (Among the great players the one extreme is represented by Enesco, who played with almost no tightening, the other extreme by Kreisler, who tightened the bow-hair to about $\frac{1}{2}$ inch from the stick at mid-point.)

Under these given conditions a steady tone on the violin can only be achieved by constant changes and adjustments between the various units of the bowing mechanism.

Generally, the length of the violin bow is about 29 inches, its weight can vary between 53 and 63 grams, about 2 ounces, more or less. This latter information seems to surprise most young violinists, who usually think that the bow is much heavier. It only feels that way, as any long object does when held at one end. This misconception often accounts for too tight a grip on the bow.

To create the sound, the bow is drawn across the strings at various speeds and pressures. The resulting friction, caused partly by microscopic hooks protruding from the hair-strands, makes the strings vibrate. These vibrations are amplified and made audible by the air enclosed in the body of the violin, which serves as a resonance box, and transmitted from the string to the top and back of the violin through the bridge and soundpost.

Each of the three main parts of the bow-arm has its distinct role in moving the bow, even in combination with the others. These sections diminish in length (as well as in muscle-strength) from the shoulder down: the upper arm is longest, followed by the somewhat shorter forearm, and the much shorter hand with its subdivisions, the even shorter fingers. Of these, the thumb is further divided into two phalanges, the others into three.

The sections of the bow-arm can act separately or in combination, giving several units of different lengths and in effect constituting a multi-sectioned pendulum. Since the speed of the pendulum's movements or oscillations depends on its length (the longer, the slower) the length of the arm-unit(s) has to be adjusted to the speed of the bow-stroke, and co-ordinated with the bow-amount. The faster the stroke (détaché or spiccato), the shorter the arm-unit and bow-length to be used. As a general rule: very fast strokes = hand motion, very small bow-amount, in the middle or upper half of the bow; moderate speeds = hand + forearm motion, greater amount of bow in the middle or upper half; slow tempo, long notes = whole bow, whole-arm movement (hand + forearm + upper arm).

The various sections of the arm consist of rigid bones and flexible muscles, tendons and ligaments, and are connected to each other by joints. Both as a whole unit and in its separate parts the arm is moved by flexing and extending the muscles, which are also capable of rotating each section (except the fingers) around its axis.

The joints permit considerable independence of movement to the individual sections of the arm besides attaching them to each other. It is extremely important to realize, however, that the *joints cannot initiate motion*. They can only react to outside forces, such as muscle contractions or extensions. Since these actions by the muscles involved cannot be seen, and only the resulting bending of the wrist or elbow is visible, it is easy to conclude, mistakenly, that the joints originate these motions. They must be flexible in order to react and adapt to the motions of the sections which they connect, but to move the bow in its normal directions by the wrist, elbow or shoulder *alone* is not possible. Failure to understand this leads to misconceptions about the role and capabilities of the joints and explains a number of well-intentioned but misleading instructions.

What is commonly called a 'wrist' motion, is in reality either:

(1) A hand motion, initiated and carried out by the hand, where the fingertip end of the hand moves most, up and down, sideways or in circles, and the forearm motion, if any, remains secondary. You can see this for yourself by holding the forearm just below the wrist with your left hand and moving the right hand in various directions.

or:

(2) A forearm motion, where the forearm initiates and makes the movements with very little hand motion. This you can see by holding your right-hand fingertips steady and moving your forearm up or down, sideways or in circles.

You can also demonstrate this forearm motion by placing a coin on the top of your right hand and moving the forearm in various directions— keeping the top of your hand parallel to the floor—without dropping the coin.

In both of these movements the wrist has an important but passive role: it reacts to motions originating on either side of it, adjusting to the changing angles and ensuring the flexibility of the moving parts. To fulfil this role, the wrist should be kept in a 'neutral' position, from which it can bend in any direction: neither too low (especially at the tip) nor too high (especially at the frog). Although the fingers are capable of independent action, thanks to their own set of muscles, and can move the bow by themselves within a very limited range, their role is also mostly passive. Reacting as springs, they ensure flexibility and continuity in bow-changes, elasticity in spiccato, fine-tuning bow-articulation and helping in the control of bow-direction. In their limited *active* role they can add extra speed to the bow for short distances, help in string crossings and balance the bow at the frog with the little finger. Although very important, these are correcting, secondary actions, not to be confused with the primary, basic function of moving the bow.

The muscles vary in strength according to which section of the arm they belong: they are strongest in the upper arm and less strong towards the fingers. As in any sporting activity, no matter how much skill it requires, the best results are obtained—often with the least physical effort—by using muscles which in their strength are proportionate to the task. This crucial correlation is too often ignored, notably by overloading the small finger muscles with too heavy a burden, such as using too much finger-pressure in tone-production.

Such misuse of the muscles causes stiffness which tends to spread to other parts of the body, often resulting in tendonitis and other physical ailments. This is becoming more and more prevalent in our already stressful times, leading to the rise of musicians' clinics and physicians specializing in these ailments. As elsewhere in medicine, an ounce of prevention is worth a long, expensive cure.

TRIPLET/GRACE NOTES — V. SHORT MOVEMENT
MIDDLE OR TIP OF BOW -
HAND

INCREASING WEIGHT - USE ARM NOT FINGERS OR
HAND

2 HOLDING THE BOW

The manner of holding the bow is of such fundamental importance that it is no exaggeration to say that there can be no successful or advanced bow technique without a correct, efficient and relaxed bow-hold. The hand itself is a marvel of ingenuity, flexibility and mobility, with fingers built and set in an ideal way to hold the bow (although, obviously, it is the bow which is built to fit the hand) and to produce sound with it from the violin.

The bow is held by applying gentle and equal pressure from the four fingers on one side of the stick against the thumb on the opposite side. The correct placement of all the fingers is important, but that of the thumb is critical. It should be <u>placed on the stick in the small space between the ridge of the frog and the leather grip</u> and in such a way that only the inside, upper corner of its fingertip (very close to the edge of the fingernail) touches the stick. This will preserve the natural position of the thumb vis-a-vis the other fingers and will bend in the direction of the bow's motion.

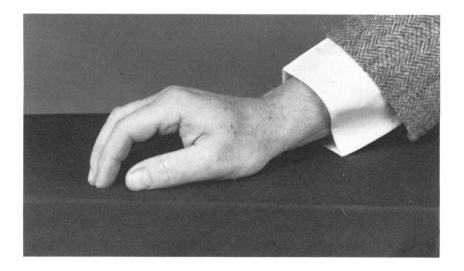

As a test, place your hand on the table, with the four fingers curved, palm downward: you will see that the thumb is set in on its edge—sideways, not fully facing the other fingers. Yet many violinists twist their thumb around when holding the bow and placing the whole surface of its fingertip flat on the stick. This is an unnatural, stressful position—just try to twist your thumb around without the bow!—in which the thumb does not bend in the direction of the bow, works against the other fingers instead of with them and is the cause of an insecure bow-hold. Sensing this, the player is forced to grip the bow too hard and yet has the feeling that the bow will drop at any moment.

Another seemingly minor, yet very important and often overlooked condition of a secure and effortless bow-hold is the extent of the space between the leather grip and the ridge of the frog. When the bow-hair is stretched to its playing tension, this space should be about $\frac{1}{4}$ of an inch, just so that the thumb can lean against both and get support from either side. If this space is too wide or too small, or if the leather grip is worn off, there is nothing to prevent the thumb from slipping, giving the player the same sense of insecurity. A good way of testing that the space is correct is to loosen the bow-hair completely and to make sure that the grip and the frog just touch. When having your bow rehaired, insist that this condition is met and have the leather grip replaced before it begins to wear off.

The forefinger and the little finger should be placed on the stick at an approximately equal distance from the thumb's contact point. The tip of the little finger rests on the top, flat section of the octagonal surface (all bow-sticks are octagonal at the frog) opposite the outer edge of the frog. The forefinger joins the bow just above the upper edge of the bow-grip; the point of contact on the finger itself depends on the different bow-holds of the various 'schools' of violin playing. Forming a triangle with the thumb, which acts as the fulcrum, both fingers have sufficient distance from it for the needed leverage in various dynamics: the forefinger transfers power from the forearm muscles by inward rotation (positive pressure) for the louder passages, the little finger by outward rotation (negative pressure) for the softer ones.

The middle and ring-fingers are placed flat on the outer side of the frog, the tip of the middle finger reaching the bottom edge of it (or close to it) and the ring-finger slightly higher. These fingers support the bow from the side opposite the thumb, and they can reinforce either the forefinger or the little finger in their various tasks.

In applying the inward-rotating, positive pressure, the forefinger should act as the extension of the forearm, not as a substitute for it. It should transmit, but not originate the pressure which, especially in the higher dynamic range, would be too great an effort for its relatively small muscles. In this the forefinger should not act independently of the forearm.

The little finger should serve as the extension of the forearm for outward-rotating, negative pressure, reducing bow-pressure on the string; but as this requires far less strength than positive pressure, it can also act independently in this task.

There should be a small space between the four fingers, otherwise there is a likelihood of sideways, squeezing pressure between them, causing too tight a grip, loss of flexibility and waste of energy. If either the forefinger or the little finger is too close to the thumb, they will have a loss of leverage as well. The extent of pressure applied in holding the bow should be adjusted to dynamics and bowing types, greater in f (such as chords), lesser in p (such as spiccato). In any case, it should not be more than the minimum needed for a secure but elastic bow-hold.

Players trying to get a 'big sound' from finger-pressure alone, instead of using the bigger muscles, end up forcing the fingers into a tight bow-grip where most of the effort is wasted in squeezing the bow-stick. Without the necessary power, or the use of leverage in its transmission, this has little effect on tone production other than producing a very ugly and unpleasant sound.

The thumb has the versatility to provide the counterpressure to both the forefinger and the little finger, to act as the fulcrum of the lever transmitting both the positive or negative pressure, and to furnish the countersupport to the two middle fingers. The thumb can also assist the forefinger and the little finger in their additional roles as rudders: it acts again as the fulcrum—this time as a horizontal one—as the fingers change or correct the direction of the bow, steering it away from, or toward the bridge. Note that the two fingers work in opposite directions: one pushes while the other pulls.

The most obvious difference between the so-called 'schools' of violin playing lies in where the forefinger comes into contact with the bow-stick. In the 'German' school (Joachim, Sevcik) the forefinger touches the stick in its nail-joint; in the 'Russian' (Auer, Heifetz, Milstein), at or near the base joint, and in the 'Franco-Belgian' (Ysaye, Kreisler, Thibaud), at the middle joint. There are also various branches and combinations of these schools (Hubay, Flesch, Galamian) where the borderlines fade or overlap. These bow-holds do have an impact, in a general way, on the musical and technical characteristics of players belonging to the various schools: the great flexibility but moderate carrying power of the German school; the very large tone but less flexibility of the Russian, and a combination of the two attributes of the Franco-Belgian. Whatever your affiliation, remember that the pivotal position of the thumb is all-important for freedom of motion and flexibility in all fingers.

Excessive finger-action is not only unnecessary, but detrimental to an efficient bow technique. Nevertheless, the fingers must constantly be in a state of flexible alertness, ready to act or react instantly. To develop and maintain their suppleness, the following exercises will be useful:

(1)   Without the bow:

    (a)   Stretch out all fingers, forming a continuous straight line with the top of the hand; palm facing down.

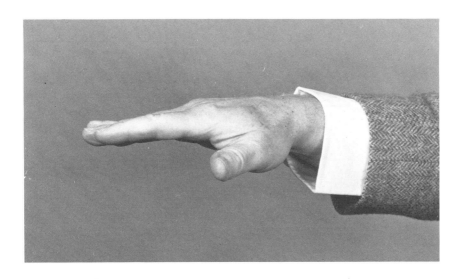

    (b)   Bend the four fingers (without the thumb) downwards, from the base knuckle only, to form a 90° angle with the top of the hand.

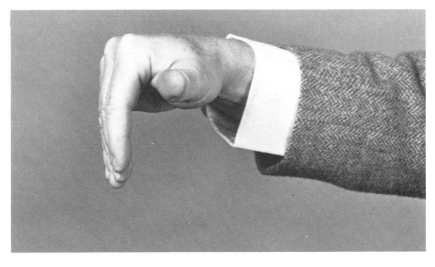

(c) Curl the four fingers tightly upwards until the fingertips touch the top edge of the palm and the first phalanges form a straight line with the top of the hand. Repeat several times.

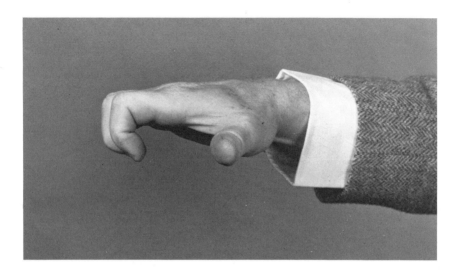

(2) Imagining the bow in hand:

(a) Place the upper, inner tip of the thumb against the middle finger between its middle and nail phalanges.

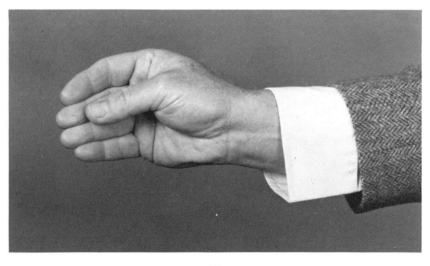

(b) Maintaining contact with the thumb, bend and straighten it and the fingers in and out several times.

(c) Pick up a pencil, hold it as if it were a bow, and do the same.

(3) With the bow in hand:

(a) Hold it in a normal playing position horizontally in front of you, without the violin, supporting the tip with the top of your left hand, and repeat the bending-stretching motions as above. This should move the bow for a short distance in its regular up-bow, down-bow direction.
(b) Hold the bow vertically, tip pointing upwards without left-hand support, and repeat the previous motions.
(c) Hold the bow again horizontally, as when playing on the violin, but without the left-hand support, and repeat the above motions. Do each of these exercises several times.

In actual playing, the fingers are in their extreme bent position at the frog, stretching out *gradually* to their full length upon reaching the tip. They adjust to the changing angle formed by the bow and the bow-arm in order to maintain contact with the bow-stick. The little finger often has an active role in the lower half of the bow: by pressing downwards on the frog-end of the bow (using the thumb as fulcrum), it can reduce the bow-pressure on the string, counter-balance the weight of the arm, and offset the tendency toward an involuntary crescendo when approaching the frog. This downward pressure by the little finger (a vertical action) is possible only by extension from a curved position and requires muscle strength. The following exercises will be helpful in developing it:

(1)   Without the violin:

   (a)   Hold the bow as if it were near the frog on the G string, the little finger (and the others) bent.

   (b)   Extend the little finger slowly, using the thumb as fulcrum, and press the frog-end downward until it reaches the E string level, raising the tip at the same time. Use the little finger alone in this, without turning the hand or forearm, and keep the top of the hand parallel to the floor.

   (c)   Just as slowly, bend the little finger gradually and let the tip of the bow descend by it own weight, raising the frog back to the G string level. Do not turn the hand.

(2)   With the violin:

(a)   Place the bow on the G string about $1\frac{1}{2}$ inches from the frog, so as to leave enough room to reach the E string without any horizontal movement by the bow as you cross the strings.

(b)   Repeat the above exercises with the bow on the strings.

By strengthening the base muscle of the little finger, its tendency to slip off the stick will also be minimized.

While excessive finger-action is unnecessary, inadequate use of it is even more detrimental to an effective bow technique. This is especially noticeable at or near the frog, where, quite often, instead of being bent, the fingers are still stiffly extended. In this position they cannot act as shock-absorbers, cannot ensure a 'smooth ride' for the bow and flexibility and tone quality suffer.

Another frequent problem connected with right-hand finger-action is that instead of a gradual bending from tip to frog, most of it is done suddenly near or at the frog, at the end of the up-bow. This causes an acceleration of the bow, resulting in an unwanted accent and a too-noticeable bow-change. These difficulties might partially explain why so many violinists are reluctant to use the vicinity of the frog, depriving themselves of a valuable area of expressive tonal resource by using, in effect, a considerably shortened bow.

The above exercises should solve these problems, increase your freedom of action and prevent predicaments associated with a sense of insecurity and stage-fright.

3 MOVING THE BOW

The bow in motion involves the bowing arm, the violin, as held by the left arm, and the bow itself. As various conditions change in this unit (such as dynamics, speed and amount of bow), so do all the interconnecting parts, and any change involves a whole series of consequent changes. To be in complete command, the player must understand these relationships and keep them in mind. Instead of taking them for granted, violinists should periodically review and practise even the most elementary principles, just as golfers and tennis players do with the basics of their game. (The great cellist, Pablo Casals, for example, practised open strings for hours on end.)

One of the basic goals of string playing is to draw a steady, even tone from the instrument. The first condition for this is that the bow has to move parallel to the bridge, that is, at a constant distance from it, and at right angles to the strings. In order to maintain this direction, the player also has to consider the angle at which the violin is held to the chest (normally ca. 45°) as well as its plane, its tilt to the right. (This tilt of the violin should be slight, otherwise the bow operates mostly on the side of the violin instead of on top of it, thereby loosening its solid support and secure base, and distorting all dynamic (pressure) and mechanical (directional) relationships. Players using a shoulder-pad should be doubly careful not to exaggerate this tilt.)

The path of the bow must also remain on the same plane as the string on which it moves, in order not to touch the neighbouring strings. The distance, or tolerance, between these planes is very small when playing at the frog, but increases as you approach the tip, due to the divergent inclinations:

G STRING
D STRING
A STRING
E STRING

The second condition for a steady, even tone of the same dynamic level is that there has to be a constant and even pressure from the *bow* to the *string*, which in turn requires constant change and adjustment in the *arm-pressure* to the *bow*.

The third basic condition for a steady tone is steady and constant bow-speed. (Under ideal circumstances, all three of these conditions are present; since this is not always the case, an advanced bow technique should be capable of producing an even tone under various circumstances.)

Starting the down-bow at the frog, it is the upper arm, as part of the whole arm, which initiates the movement. Due to the given direction the bow has to follow, it is the only part of the arm which at that point can move the bow straight and parallel to the bridge for any length. The forearm, near the frog, can only move the bow away from, or toward the bridge by itself; the hand, on its own, would cause a sideways motion; the wrist can only react to movements of the hand or forearm, and the fingers can move the bow only a very short distance by themselves.

Continuing the down-bow in its straight path toward the middle of the bow, the upper arm remains in control for a while, but gradually the forearm takes over (the upper arm being no longer capable of moving the bow straight). Around mid-point, depending on the length of the player's bow-arm, it begins its primary role in moving the bow and keeps it until the tip. In the up-bow the reverse occurs and for the same reason: the forearm starts the motion at the tip and the upper arm, taking over around mid-point, guides the bow straight to the frog. The conclusion to be drawn from these actions is that the *lower half* of the bow is controlled by the *upper arm*, and the *upper half* by the *forearm*. Remember this rule whenever you need to solve a problem at any part of the bow.

In fast, short strokes the hand is the primary mover of the bow. Being the shortest of the three main arm units, it is best suited to rapid motions in keeping with the rule of the pendulum. Hand motion is often and incorrectly called a wrist motion. While flexible, the role of the wrist is passive and secondary to the hand.

The level of the arm should be, with very few exceptions, the same as that of the bow. Starting the down-bow at the frog, the upper arm should follow the same inclination as the bow path, depending on which string the bow moves. If not, a sudden drop of the elbow will be needed to bring the upper arm back in line with the bow. This creates an overload of pressure on the bow, forcing it to rebound skittishly. Likewise, a difference of height will be created between high elbow and low bow-level if, at the tip, the up-bow starts by raising the upper arm instead of using the forearm. The result will be a decrease of pressure, having the same effect as the soft pedal on the piano. Too low an arm position will always limit freedom of action and inhibit boldness and incisiveness in bow-handling.

Suggestions for Practice (photocopy)

The following exercise using Kreutzer's sixth and seventh Etudes can be relied upon to discover and correct such flaws; practise with whole-bow martelé strokes; move the bow full-length as rapidly and lightly as possible, making each note very short but the rests between the note quite long, so that the tempo of the piece remains very slow. A steady, unshaking bow is proof that your bow-arm is moving correctly. If your bow bounces, or if the tone is very rough, reduce the pressure at the frog and correct the rate of ascent and descent until your arm follows the path of the bow:

No.6 (42 Studies)   *Kreutzer*

No.7 (42 Studies)   *Kreutzer*

In two exceptions to this rule, the upper arm is higher than the bow-level: in spiccato bowing the height differential makes the bow bounce, this time deliberately and under control, as when bouncing a rubber ball; and in preparation for crossing strings from E or A to the G string, very frequent in such chordal passages as:

Sonata No.2: Allemande   *Bach*

Players with shorter arms may need an additional, slight arm-movement near the tip, which is seldom noticed. In the upper half of the down-bow their forearm may be fully extended before reaching the tip. In order to use the whole bow and to continue it in a straight line, the upper arm (most noticeably at the elbow) may have to be moved inward, extending the arm's reach. Just as importantly, the reverse of this motion must start the up-bow at the tip, moving the upper arm (elbow) slightly outward *horizontally*. Without it, the bow will not move straight, but curve away from the bridge. This motion is not to be confused with the faulty, premature *raising* of the elbow at the beginning of the up-bow, which is a *vertical* motion.

If this extra movement still does not lead to a straight bow-path, change slightly the angle at which you hold the violin, either by moving the scroll-end of it inward, to the right, or by moving the chinrest end farther to the left, outward on your shoulder. This latter solution is usually more successful and needs no change in the left arm position, although it may require a different chinrest.

Tall players with long arms might find it easier to draw the bow straight by moving either the scroll further to the left, or the chinrest end further to the right.

The bow moves parallel to the bridge, usually at an equal distance, while the dynamic level remains the same. At other times, changes in dynamics or tone colour, different bow-speed, length of bow-stroke or playing in very high positions make it necessary to move the bow closer or farther away from the bridge. The rule of friction is that any change in the right angles formed by the bow-direction and the string will force the bow either away from, or towards the bridge. This is a natural tendency, occurring spontaneously, which can be counteracted by opposing pressure, but which can also be used to change the distance from the bridge when necessary.

Specifically, if the bow is slanted so that the frog-end is closer to the bridge and the tip further away, a down-bow stroke will force the bow away from the bridge and an up-bow closer to it; when the bow is slanted in the opposite direction, the down-bow stroke will push it closer and the up-bow further away from the bridge:

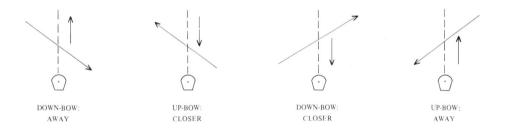

| DOWN-BOW: | UP-BOW: | DOWN-BOW: | UP-BOW: |
| AWAY | CLOSER | CLOSER | AWAY |

The optimum distance of the bow from the bridge is a certain fraction of the whole vibrating string-length, which diminishes when the left hand is in the higher positions. Not adjusting the bow's location to this change is often the cause of unpleasant tone quality when playing in the higher positions.

To test and illustrate the straightness of the bow-path and the overall correctness of moving the bow:

(1)   Hold the violin normally.
(2)   Ask a friend or your teacher to place the bow-tip on a string, holding the bow parallel to the bridge.
(3)   Place your right hand at the tip and hold the stick as if you were holding it at the frog.
(4)   Move your hand and arm up and down, keeping contact the whole length of the bow-stick, which is being held stationary by the other person.

This way you will know that your arm moves in a straight line and it will be easier to visualize and control the correct motions. Try to memorize the muscular feeling of these movements, which can then be recalled and duplicated during actual playing.

CHANGING THE BOW

A seamless, unnoticeable bow-change, like a singer's breath-control, is essential for an uninterrupted, beautiful singing tone, giving the impression of an unlimited bow-supply and an unending bow. This is no easy task: the bow, arriving at the end of a stroke, has to reverse direction and return on the same track; reversing the direction means a momentary halt; without bow-motion there is no sound, without sound no continuity of tone or phrasing.

The only way to avoid this gap is to maintain the continuous motion of the bow, even if at a reduced speed. This can be done by moving it in a 'loop' with a flat elliptical path at the moment of bow-change. The loop can be either horizontal or vertical:

But if you use the vertical loop, it should be flat enough so as not to touch the neighbouring strings. While guiding the bow in this loop, the actions of the various parts of the arm are staggered: they change direction consecutively, one slightly after the other. This principle of de-synchronization is the same as in walking: one leg moves forward while the other is already preparing the next step in a continuous, overlapping motion. The swimmer's crawl-stroke is an even more closely related comparison to our bow-change motions.

Suggestions for Practice

For a smooth bow-change from up- to down-bow in the lower half, practise the following procedure in slow motion: just before the end of the up-bow stroke, start a slight downward motion with the upper arm and turn it gradually into the down-bow path, while the hand is still finishing its up-bow motion and is straightening gently from its slightly bent position. When the rest of the arm is joined in this way in the down-bow motion, the slight delay allows the fingers to complete their bending movement smoothly and to conclude the up-bow motion of the bow itself. By then the arm is on its way in the down-bow stroke, moving momentarily, in effect, in the opposite direction from the fingers and the bow, which are just finishing the loop.

For changing the bow from down-bow to up-bow, simply reverse the direction of the movements in the sequence: while in the up-down change it is basically clockwise, in the down-up change it is mostly counter-clockwise.

Note that the finger-movements are passive: they react to motions by other parts of the arm and are last to complete the change. Sudden, excessive finger movements just before the change speed up the bow, and the added speed causes the unwanted accent which one tries to avoid for a smooth, unnoticeable bow-change. To counteract the tendency for this speed-up, practise changing the bow very slowly, reducing the bow-speed even further just before the change. Bow-change can be a greater problem in the lower half or near the frog, where the greater weight and somewhat crowded position of the arm may aggravate and magnify any imperfection. A smooth bow change is especially important when it occurs in the middle of a phrase, otherwise the phrasing is altered.

STRING CROSSING

String-crossing in legato is somewhat similar to bow-change in its dual phrasing possibilities. Notes can be bound together under a slur or articulated at the point of change by the manner in which the strings are crossed, and this is also a musical decision.

Preparation, or anticipation, is the key to smooth legato string-crossings and to even passages of scales and arpeggios in any tempo. The bow should move in an uninterrupted arc, approaching the next string gradually during the last notes on the previous string. In this motion it is led, and slightly preceded by the bow-arm. The left-hand fingers must also anticipate: the finger due on the next string should be put down before the bow gets there. In scales this usually involves the first and little finger: both should be placed on the neighbouring strings in a double-stop. This way the bow does not have to hesitate before the crossing (nor will the scale have a 'missing tooth') and can continue uninterrupted on its arc, contributing to the evenness of the passage.

If the musical context calls for an articulated string crossing, the path of the bow will be more angular, resembling a staircase: and the articulation will be the result of the sudden drop or rise in the bow-level from one string to the other.

Crossing the strings from the G string towards the E string down-bow, and from the E string towards the G string up-bow is a more natural movement for the bow-arm and more advantageous for the bow than the other way around. In this direction, every time the bow goes from one string to the next, you gain a length of bow-hair equivalent to the distance between two strings. To prove this, start the down-bow at the frog on the G string towards the E string, using only as much bow-length on each string as the distance separating them: you will still be at the frog when reaching the E string. Going in the opposite direction, up-bow from G to E string, you will lose the same amount of bow. Therefore, whenever possible, use down-bow for up-scale passages, up-bow for down-scale passages.

When string-crossing in a legato passage involves only one note on another string, followed by a return to the original string, wavy, vertical hand-motion should be used. (Remember that the shorter the motion, the shorter the arm-unit). This is especially true if the same motion keeps recurring, as in bariolage (= mixing two or more strings):

Sonata No.3: first movement   *Brahms*

In détaché string-crossing the same applies: the faster the bow-speed, the shorter the arm-unit:

Partita No.3: Preludium   *Bach*

The vertical hand-motion used in string-crossing is in addition to, and in combination with the horizontal up- and down-bow motion of the forearm or upper arm, depending on the bow-length and the section of the bow used: forearm for the short détaché strokes, and both forearm and whole arm for the long, whole-bow strokes.

When string-crossing involves three or four strings, however, the short range of the hand alone cannot cover the distance between the outer strings and an additional string-crossing motion from the upper arm is needed. This motion of the upper arm (usually in short détaché strokes in the middle or upper half of the bow) is strictly away from and toward the body and must not be part of the horizontal, up-bow down-bow motion of the forearm. The whole arm, combined into one motion and used as a rigid unit, would be too long for even moderately fast détaché string-crossings and could not guide the bow in a straight line.

The three units of the arm, helped by the flexibility of the joints, must perform their different tasks independently:

(1) the upper arm vertically, across the strings,
(2) the forearm horizontally in the up-bow and down-bow motion of the détaché,
(3) the hand, assisting in both directions.

The mixing of these three motions into one stiff movement is one of the most frequent faults of bow technique, and will lead to stiffness and frustration if uncorrected.

Suggestions for Practice

To avoid or correct this mistake in the détaché crossing of several strings, practise the following exercises:

(1) Without the bow:
    (a) hold your bow-arm at string level as if playing in the middle of the bow; move your forearm back and forth in a détaché stroke without moving the upper arm;
    (b) lower your upper arm from the E string level next to your body without any forearm motion, and raise it back again several times;
    (c) move both units together, raising and lowering the upper arm slowly while moving the forearm horizontally and somewhat more rapidly.

(2) With the bow:
    Practise various string-crossing patterns on open strings:

Then practise this pattern in Bach's 'Preludium'

A E A D Strings

on open strings without the left hand, starting with each of the four strings and with various rhythms:

35

In the next example a fourth motion joins the other three: the fingers bend and stretch more actively than usual in order to keep all the bow-hair flat on the string (also used in the 'Preludium' and similar instances):

No.13 (42 Studies)   *Kreutzer*

In general, practise complicated string-crossings reduced to their open-string patterns by leaving out the left-hand fingers. In this way it is possible to concentrate on one difficulty at a time and to visualize the particular bow-pattern:

Preludium and Allegro   *Kreisler*

Sonata No.3: first movement   *Beethoven*

DISTRIBUTING THE BOW

The ideal condition for obtaining an even tone during various bowings is when the amount of bow available is proportionate to the time-value of the stroke:

(a)

WHOLE BOW   HALF BOWS   WHOLE BOW   HALF BOWS

(b)

NOT IDEAL   BETTER

(c)

In the last example the ratio of the time-values is 3:1, that is consequently the ratio of the bow-amounts should be the same. If the bow is divided mentally into three equal parts, the first down-bow uses the whole bow, the next up-bow the upper third; the following down-bow uses the same upper third, returning to the tip for the next up-bow whole bow:

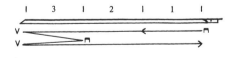

A more complicated example is found in Bach's original bowing:

Sonata No.1: last movement   *Bach*

Dividing the length of the bow-hair into 12 equal parts, start in the middle of
the bow (section 7) and use one unit for each of the first four détaché notes,
three units for the three legato notes in the next down-bow (sections 7–9) and
six units for the following up-bow (9–4); one unit again for each of the next
three détaché notes (4) followed by a three-unit up-bow (4–2) and conclude
with the six-unit down-bow (2–7), which leads back to the starting point: (you
could also start in unit 8, keeping the action farther from the frog)

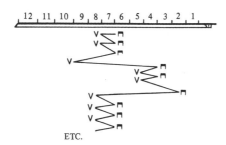

Disproportionate bow-lengths can often be corrected and equalized by
attaching shorter note-values to either end of a longer stroke, but preserving
the original phrasing (divided into 16 equal parts, $\eighthnote = 1$, $\quarternote = 2$):

Sonata No.3: last movement   *Bach*

Equalized bowing:

Original bowing:

The total note-value of the stroke determines the number of bow-length units
to be used. Otherwise, either the separate notes would get three times as much
bow-amount, speed and sound-volume (accent) as the five slurred notes, or,
using proportionate bow-lengths, you would run out of bow, losing space
toward the tip:

equalised bowing:

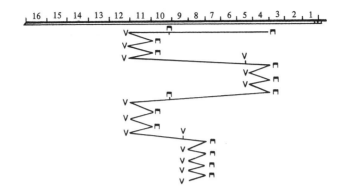

but with the original bowing:

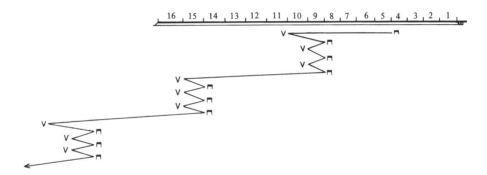

When the uneven distribution of the bow-length is unavoidable, bow-speed, bow-amount, pressure and distance from the bridge have to be so mixed as to produce the evenness of tone and careful phrasing which the musical context requires. Two examples illustrate this:

(1)   Even distribution:

(2)   Uneven distribution:

Suggestions for Practice

To practise even bow-speed and equal bow-distribution:

(1) divide the bow-stick (i.e. the length of hair) into three, four, six or eight equal parts by light chalk-marks;
(2) move the bow on an open string in equal ♩s with the metronome set at ♩ = 60, trying to cross each chalk-mark exactly at the sound of each beat:

(3) repeat in different division units and at various metronome settings.

In any combination or distribution of bow-speed, bow-amount, pressure and location, you have to consider yet another element of lesser, but not negligible importance: the tilting of the bow-stick. This controls the thickness of bow-hair that is applied to the string and which varies according to circumstances. As a rule, you should use only part of the hair strands in *p*, at greater bow-speeds and in most off-string bowings to give the bow more elasticity and sensitivity. Tilt the bow-stick away from the bridge by rolling it between the fingers, *not* by turning the hand and forcing the wrist too high. In *f* use the full hair with the stick directly above it; this will give more surface contact and greater volume. It is very important not to tilt the stick too much in *f* passages of slow bow-speed: the vertical force of the added pressure would press the tilted stick into the string, creating a scraping, rasping sound.

4 CHECK-LIST I

(1)   Be sure that in holding the bow the thumb is in its natural position, on its edge, not twisted around to face the fingers.

(2)   Do not hold the bow by the fingertips—the middle fingers should be resting flat on the lower part of the frog.

(3)   Bend and extend the fingers gradually between the tip and the frog.

(4)   The little finger should touch the stick opposite the end of the frog, at the same distance from the thumb as the forefinger.

(5)   The fingers should be spaced slightly apart, not squeezed together.

(6)   Hold the bow no tighter than necessary at any dynamic level.

(7)   Keep the wrist near its middle position as much as possible—avoid extreme flexing or bending at the tip or at the frog.

(8)   Be clear about hand-motion and forearm motion: neither is wrist motion.

(9)   Tilt the bow-stick slightly away from the bridge in p, but keep the stick directly above the bow-hair in f—avoid pressing the stick into the string.

(10)   Move the bow parallel to the bridge whenever possible.

(11)   Move the bow at an appropriate distance from the bridge, adjusted for bow-speed and pressure for good tone quality.

(12)   Use the appropriate section of your arm, and in the correct bow-section at any bow-speed.

(13)   Keep the elbow on the same plane as the bow, maintaining the same level territory between the arm and the bow (except in spiccato).

(14)   Make sure that the arm (elbow) follows the same incline in its rise and descent as the bow.

(15)   Avoid too much finger-action (and bow speed-up) in bow-change.

(16)   Keep an even tone during bow-change.

(17)   In all détaché string-crossings keep the forearm and upper-arm motions distinct and independent; do not mix them into one rigid whole-arm motion.

(18)   Prepare your string-crossings in legato; move the bow in a continuous arc; cross step-wise for articulation only.

(19)   Use bow-amount proportionate to time-value whenever possible.

(20)   Practise complicated string-crossing patterns on open strings.

5 PRODUCING GOOD TONE

There are two aspects to tone production: the mechanical and the physiological. The bow provides the first, the player the second.

Mechanically, there are three main elements:

(1) bow-speed
(2) bow-pressure
(3) distance from the bridge.

The three are interdependent. They change in proportion to each other but their sum total remains constant on a given, steady dynamic level. If the bow-speed is increased, the bow-pressure should be reduced and the distance of the bow from the bridge changed (in this instance increased) in order to maintain the same dynamic level. With decreased speed the opposite is true, so that the following rules may be observed:

(1) The greater the bow-speed,
     the lesser the bow-pressure,
     the greater the distance from the bridge.

(2) The lesser the bow-speed,
     the greater the bow-pressure,
     the lesser the distance from the bridge.

Bow-speed and bow-pressure are inversely proportionate at the same dynamic level, and the distance of the bow from the bridge depends on their interrelation.

The following schema illustrates the various mixtures on three different dynamic levels, although a sphere, like a balloon blown up into three different sizes, would be a truer image, corresponding to piano, mezzo-forte and forte.

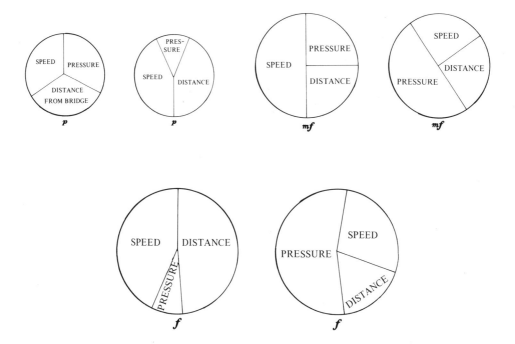

For any change in the dynamic level of the sound, speed or pressure can be increased or decreased, and for a very great or sudden rise or drop in dynamic level both can be increased or decreased together. The distance of the bow from the bridge has to be adjusted accordingly: too much bow-pressure too far from the bridge will cause the tone to crack, especially at very low speeds, the resistance of the string being too weak at that point. Too little pressure too close to the bridge, especially at greater bow-speeds, will result in 'ponticello' sound, the string being too taut at that point to vibrate fully without considerable bow-pressure.

It is important to distinguish and differentiate between the pressure that the bow exerts on the string ('weight' or 'gravity') and the pressure that the player applies to the bow ('force' or 'power'). Confusing these two concepts can create a number of problems, stemming from the uniform use of the word 'pressure' in expressing widely divergent notions.

To maintain the same dynamic level at a given steady bow-speed, the pressure *by the bow on the string* must remain the same along the length of the bow from frog to tip. To maintain this same pressure, however, the force exerted *by the arm on the bow* must be changing: increasing from the frog to the tip and decreasing from the tip to the frog. The force that causes the bow to depress the string and the physical change that the string experiences as a result, is the consequence of the combined weight of the bow itself (greatest at the frog, lightest at the tip) and the power of the arm-pressure.

At the frog, the hand, being right above the contact point between bow and string, can exert the weight of the arm directly on the string. Moving away from the frog, however, the distance between the point of the power's origin in the arm and the contact point between the bow and the string, where it needs to be transferred, becomes greater. Transmission of power over this distance can only be effected by the leverage of opposing forces between the thumb and the forefinger. To increase the pressure in the down-bow from frog to tip, the forearm, hand and forefinger turn inward, counter-clockwise *as a unit*, while the thumb, as part of the same motion, turns and presses upward against the downward pressure of the forefinger. To decrease the pressure in the up-bow, the reverse procedure will apply: starting at the tip with the same increased pressure achieved at the end of the down-bow, the inward torque-power is gradually reduced by the outward, clockwise turning of the forearm and hand unit, this time using the little finger as their representative on the bow-stick. Arriving back at the frog, the intial weight-pressure ratio is regained.

ARM

FOREFINGER

THUMB

POSITIVE PRESSURE
INWARD ROTATION (COUNTER-CLOCKWISE)

ARM

LITTLE FINGER

THUMB

NEGATIVE PRESSURE
OUTWARD ROTATION

The bow-stick serves as the axis and the thumb as the fulcrum around which these changes of power occur. Although the player experiences the feeling of increasing pressure in the forefinger, which is in direct contact with the bow, the force must come from the forearm muscle, which alone is strong enough for the task. From the player's point of view, the origin and nature of pressure progresses gradually from weight at or near the frog, to torque power towards the tip.

These relationships of power between player and bow-change vary constantly, whether the sound-volume is steady or not: a down-bow crescendo or an up-bow diminuendo requires an even greater rate of increasing or decreasing pressure. It is very seldom that we can use merely the weight of the bow to produce a satisfactory tone. That is also why using weight by itself to maintain or increase volume can work only within a minimal distance from the frog: beyond that point it has no bearing without transmission by leverage.

To test this, try to use only the weight of your arm at the tip without any lever action between thumb and forefinger: it will merely lower the bow and push the frog inward toward the violin with no effect on sound.

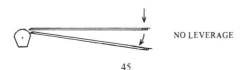

NO LEVERAGE

Another, simple experiment on a small postal balance will illustrate in a different way the consequences of using only the weight of the bow:

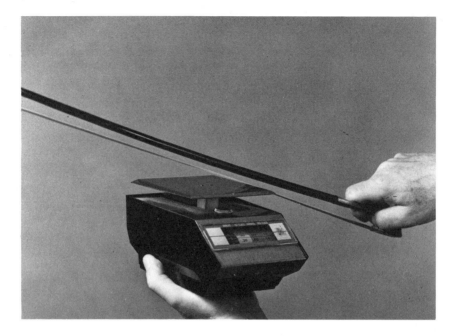

(1) Hold the balance as if it were a violin.
(2) Move the bow in a normal way on the right edge of its platform, starting at the frog and using its weight, plus a small amount of arm-weight, adding up to *c.* 4 ounces shown on the scale, equal to *mf.*
(3) Move the bow toward the tip with no increase in pressure.
(4) The amount shown on the scale will diminish until at the tip it will be no more than $\frac{1}{2}$ ounce.
(5) If you now try to maintain the same pressure at four ounces, it will be clear that considerable torque power is needed for the necessary increase in pressure.

When the inward-turning, counter-clockwise motion to increase the pressure starts at the frog, be sure that the wrist starts its bending motion (adjusting to the changing angle formed between the hand and the forearm) immediately upon leaving the frog. If this bending or lowering motion is delayed beyond the balance point of the bow, *c.* 10″ from the end of the stick, and then is done suddenly, the elasticity of the bow will cause it to 'kick back' or shake, and will make it very difficult to control. Playing with just the weight of the bow does have its usefulness, and is very effective in pianissimos and 'flautato' passages for example.

In the down-bow, maintaining the same pressure from the *arm to the bow* will *reduce* the weight (pressure) of the *bow on the string*; in the up-bow, maintaining pressure from the arm will *increase* the bow's weight on the string. Consequently, the natural way to play a diminuendo is down-bow, and a crescendo up-bow.

In the physiological aspect of string playing, as in sport or any other physical activity, the best results with the least effort are achieved by using muscles which are proportionate to the task: larger, stronger muscles for the greater physical effort, smaller ones for the more delicate actions. Trying to move a piano with the fingers alone would make no more sense than threading a needle by flexing the upper-arm muscles.

Producing a large, full sound on the violin, especially in the upper half of the bow, requires considerable physical output, as shown in the postal-balance experiment. To test this further:

(1) Hold the bow in normal playing position, but without the violin, supporting it at the tip with the left hand;

(2) Try to press the stick through the normally tightened hair, or at least until it touches the hair. The pressure must be vertical, directly into the hair, not sideways, so as not to harm the bow.

The small muscles of the fingers are inadequate for such an effort and the forefinger, which is so often and mistakenly asked to supply most of the pressure, in particular does not have the strength for the necessary torque power. This power should come from the much larger and stronger forearm muscles if you want to avoid overloading and stiffening the small muscles and the resulting strained and unpleasant sound.

When a new student auditions, one of the things that may be asked is to play a slow down-bow crescendo, starting *p* at the frog and ending *f* at the tip. When asked how it is done, the answer almost invariably is 'pressing with the forefinger'. In most cases that is precisely how it was done (with very poor results), but sometimes the same answer is given even when the player uses the larger muscles, correctly but without realizing it.

This mistake both in concept and realization is understandable when one considers that it is with the fingers that we touch and hold the bow (and the violin) and it is by the fingers that we 'feel' both the bow and the instrument. As a result, the tendency, when playing, is to concentrate all increased effort on the fingers.

There are only three contact points between the player and the instrument: the right-hand fingers to the bow, the left-hand fingers to the neck of the violin and the jaw to the chinrest and collar-bone (shoulder). Each of these involves a certain amount of pressure and counter-pressure and constitutes a mental or psychological focus, which can become the site of over-emphasis and over-exertion by the muscles directly involved. A large part of the physical and even psychological problems in string playing can be traced back to these areas.

The increased pressure which is required for a down-bow crescendo, or even for maintaining the same dynamic level between frog and tip, should come from the forearm muscles. To transmit their power to the point of contact between bow and string, the forearm, hand and fingers should be turned (rotated) inward *as a unit*, very much like turning a stubborn key in a rusty keyhole. The whole movement from frog to tip and back can also be compared to the motion of scrubbing the inside of a barrel lying on its side. It is important that after arriving at the tip with increased pressure, the up-bow should start with the same amount of pressure. A frequent mistake is to give up much of the sound during the bow-change at the tip and to start the up-bow considerably weaker than the end of the down-bow. (Another, too frequent, mistake is, of course, not to increase the pressure at all in the down-bow in the first place.)

There are a number of large muscles in the body which can be used to make violin-playing less of a physical effort and therefore more economical. The difficulty in commanding these muscles is that, contrary to the fingers, they are not in contact with the instrument and that you cannot feel their actions directly. To bring them into play and to liberate yourself from the 'fingertip' concept of tone-production requires some mental and physical practice somewhat similar to yoga. Your imagination and a few mental images are needed in order to shift the psychological focus away from the fingers and toward the larger muscles, and to approach violin-playing from a different perspective.

Violin playing is an activity in which the whole body participates—some parts more than others. The most important, directly involved large muscles are the forearm and upper-arm muscles of both arms. But others which are also very useful include, in layman's language, the right chest muscle and the back muscles, especially the area on either side of the spine, just below and inside the shoulder blades. When you succeed in letting these muscles take over most of the burden of the physical activity in violin playing, you will have freed the smaller muscles of the hand and fingers and made them available for the more delicate task of articulation, phrasing and expressive characterization.

Right-arm pressure from the bow-side should be supported and counter-balanced by the steady 'work-bench' of the violin itself, which in turn should be held by the whole left arm, especially the upper arm; do not think of it as an effort by the left hand alone. The back muscle on the right side, acting as a spiral-shaped spring, can help move the bow by contracting and pulling the bow toward the tip in down-bow, and expanding, pushing the bow toward the frog in up-bow. The back muscle on the left side can assist in holding the violin, acting like the counter-ballast in the old-fashioned lift (elevator) mechanisms.

The right chest muscle comes into play in consecutive down-bows and down-bow chords, and in starting fast, accentuated down-bows.

The following samples of mental images should help direct your attention away from the fingers to the upper arms and to the upper body itself:

(1)   You are a penguin (in tuxedo already!)—as you have flippers (upper arms) only, that is where the bow is attached and the violin held, and where all the effort is concentrated.

(2)   You are one of Siamese twins, grown together back to back; your twin is left-handed so that his/her violin is on the same side as yours. You can only play the violin if your twin plays also and all effort originates with him/her, and only when your thought-process concentrates on him/her, initiating and sparking the action.

(3)   You are a violin-playing puppet, played on in turn by the puppet-master. All effort and action comes from him—but you are both the puppet and the puppet-master.

(4)   Your chest is an accordion of which the handles are attached to the inside of your upper arms. Keeping the left arm stationary, at every down-bow your right upper arm moves away from the left arm, expanding your chest (pulling out the accordion and filling it with air); at every up-bow your right arm moves back again closer to the left arm, compressing the accordion (your chest) and pushing the air out.

(5)   You are divided vertically in two, creating contrasting halves of yourself. The two sides work not only in opposition, but also as complementary forces. The tone is the result of the two opposing forces, the left upper arm stationary, the right one mobile; the tone is not produced by one-sided pressure against a physical and mental void on the left side. (NB: In order to keep the right, mobile side of the body free at all times and the left side's resistance on a steady and firm basis, stand either with most of your weight on the left leg, or balance your body on both legs—do not stand on the right leg!)

(6)   Imagine that your back serves the same purpose as the back of the violin: it encloses it to complete the resonance box. As the air contained within the violin makes the string vibrations audible, so your upper body, and the air in your lungs, serves as a secondary resonance box, reinforcing and amplifying the sound of your violin. Without air there is no sound (as on the Moon or Mars), so make sure that your lungs are full of air. Stand tall and straight, breathe freely, and be conscious of your back muscles. Without its back the violin is just a silent practice violin; without activating your back muscles the sound-support of your violin may evaporate.

While these suggested images exist only in your imagination, they can have concrete practical results. A yogi can imagine an object of a certain weight in front of him and practise lifting it by progressively increasing its imaginary weight. Using those of his muscles which he knows are needed in lifting such a weight, he continues to increase the heaviness of this imaginary object until it reaches a certain pre-determined limit. When a real object of that weight is placed in front of him, he succeeds in lifting it in reality, having trained his muscles mentally to the task. Use your imagination the same way.

Suggestions for Practice

To develop independence of the upper-arm muscles:

(1)   Tighten the upper-arm muscles, but at the same time keep the forearm, wrist, hand and fingers totally loose and relaxed. Imagine squeezing a balloon under each upper arm and shake your hands while doing so.

(2)   Place a thick book under each arm and press them against yourself with the upper arms, letting the rest of the arm hang loosely and shaking the hand.

(3)   Remove the books and, keeping the upper-arm muscles tight, raise them slowly, together with the forearms and hands, into normal playing position. Tighten and relax the upper arms alternately without tightening the elbow, wrist or any other part of the arm or hand.

To activate the muscle on the right side of your spine just below the shoulder-blade:

(1)   Press one of your left-hand fingertips hard against the middle of this muscle and move your right arm as if you were using the whole bow. Concentrate on the muscle while moving your arm, pretending that it is a spiral-shaped spring, which contracts in the down-bow and expands in the up-bow, in effect causing and controlling the arm-motion.

(2)   To continue to 'feel' this muscle, find a corner of a piece of furniture of about equal height and, whether you are standing or sitting, lean against it with the muscle while practising. Develop this muscle until it actively takes part in moving the bow.

To involve the muscle on the left side of your back in its role of ballast and counter-support for the violin, lean back against the wall or a door, feet about 10–12 inches away from it, and play awhile in this position, concentrating on that muscle. Be aware of your back in general and keep its muscles active.

Now two playing exercises:

(1)   Play open strings with slow, whole bows, but with the forefinger off the stick and without any substitute pressure from the other fingers. Instead, make the effort from the upper arm, trying for a full sound. Use the left upper-arm resistance as the opposing force. The result should be a

very focussed, concentrated and intense sound, the vibrations of which you can feel even in the back of your head. After a while, return the forefinger to its normal position and, still using mostly the upper arm, you should get a dramatically bigger and fuller sound.

(2)   After practising this on open strings, play through some of the easier pieces in your repertoire the same way: without the forefinger at first, then normally, but with hardly any pressure from the forefinger, using mostly the upper arm. Stop and check the procedure frequently and reinforce it by mixing in a few of the upper-arm muscle-tensing exercises without the instrument. Then resume playing and enjoy the results.

This method of using bigger muscles for bigger tasks will pay a number of dividends. You will be more relaxed and better balanced physically and mentally; you will have increased energy and staying power to practise and perform for a longer time without tiring; you will be able to produce a larger, fuller and more powerful tone with less effort and force. The large muscles are also far less affected by nervousness and a bow controlled by the upper arm will not shake as a finger-controlled bow is apt to do when the player is nervous or excited. Physical and mental well-being will also reduce susceptibility to nervousness in a benign circle of one good effect inducing another. Although a thorough knowledge of a piece does wonders for self-confidence, some nervousness is likely to persist before a performance. With your new perspective, you can transform this condition into an advantage by using its energy positively, making your performance more exciting and playing at your best under all circumstances.

If some of these mental images seem rather far-fetched, it should be remembered that such a 'mind-over-matter' approach is prevalent both in sport and medicine: in the training of tennis players and basket-ball players, in preparations for the Olympics and in the treatment of patients. That most miraculous organ, the brain, is yielding more and more of its secrets to research, and even though there is still a very long way to go before we will be able to understand completely how it functions, its direct and concrete effect on our every action and reaction, and on our general well-being is already apparent and acknowledged.

Some aspects of left-hand technique, to the extent that they influence bow technique, should briefly be mentioned here. The angle which the violin forms with the player should be adjusted to the length of the player's arms, and its tilt to the right should be minimal. The scroll should be held level with the chin: if it is noticeably lower, the bow will have to operate on a sloping surface which will pull it away from the bridge. The rhythmical accuracy and articulation of the left-hand fingers are essential in both legato and détaché string-crossing. The vibrato motion should be parallel with the strings: a faulty, vertical vibrato will make the violin bob up and down at every oscillation, making the bow skip and shake on the unstable surface. Incorrect left-arm motion in shifting may also be the cause of a shaking bow, for which the player's bow-technique often and unfairly gets the blame. If in changing positions only the hand or forearm moves, the violin will be pushed up in upward shifts, and the bow with it; in down-shift, the violin drops down, away from the bow, which will then bounce after it. To avoid this, be sure that the upper arm initiates the motion and moves together with the forearm in guiding the left hand up and down the fingerboard. For proof, hold the bow with your left hand as if it were the violin and hold the frog in place on your left shoulder. Move the left hand up and down on the stick as in shifting: unless the upper arm is also moving, the tip of the bow will rise and fall with each shifting movement of hand or forearm. The correct arm-motion resembles the extension and retraction of the wall-bracket lamp:

Finally, in problematic string-crossing, decide whether the left hand or the bow-arm has the greater difficulty and choose a fingering or bowing which will help solve the bigger problem:

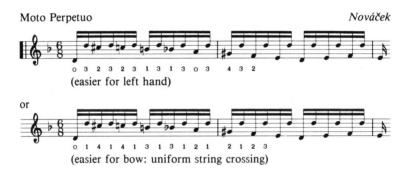

52

6   CHECK-LIST II

(1)   Use the bigger muscles for the heavier tasks (pressure).

(2)   Save the small muscles for the more delicate work (articulation).

(3)   Shift the psychological focus away from the fingers toward the bigger muscles through mental images and physical exercises.

(4)   Think of good tone as the result of opposing actions from both the left and right side.

(5)   'Pull' the sound out of the instrument, do not just 'press' it in; the pressure should also be acting horizontally, in the direction of the bow's motion, as well as vertically.

(6)   Practise drawing an even tone from frog to tip and tip to frog on open strings; learn the rate and memorize the feeling of increase and decrease in pressure needed for an even tone.

(7)   Practise slow and sustained bowing with and without the use of the forefinger.

(8)   Work toward a seamless bow-change with no loss or interruption of sound and without accents.

(9)   In shifting, move the left upper-arm together with the hand and forearm; remember that left-arm actions influence the bow-arm and tone-production as well.

(10)   Playing in a standing position, put most of your weight on the left leg, or balance your body on both legs—never put all of your weight on the right leg.

PART TWO

APPLIED
BOW TECHNIQUE

7 ARTICULATION AND PHRASING

Articulation and phrasing are the technical means by which the bow speaks intelligently and eloquently. Articulation is clarity of expression within the phrase; phrasing is clarity of thought between musical ideas.

Articulation by the bow enhances the clarity of notes within the same stroke by differentiating the dynamics through change of bow-speed and/or pressure without altering the stroke's legato character. Bow-change itself can be a natural means of articulation or phrasing, since there is a hint of separation every time we change the bow. When the bow has to be changed during the same phrase, however, the change can, and should, be made unnoticeably to preserve the phrasing.

Phrasing keeps together the notes which belong to the same musical thought and at the same time separates consecutive thoughts subtly from each other. Technically, the same variable bow-speed and intensity is used as in articulation, but in phrasing the important element of timing is often added. In speaking, we phrase by raising or lowering our voice, by slowing down or speeding up our words, and we pause between thoughts partly for clarity of meaning, partly for the need to breathe. In musical performance, where our phases also need to 'breathe', timing is a slight change in the flow of the tempo, a minimal variation in its pace either by delaying or hastening certain notes or group of notes, or by holding certain notes (or groups of notes) somewhat longer than their exact value. These agogic changes are not to be confused with *rubato*, in which we take a more pronounced liberty with tempo and rhythm.

The composer, in putting his ideas on paper, can only indicate how his music should sound—it is up to the performer to choose the appropriate technical means with which to carry out these instructions. Since it is the bow that makes the instrument sound, it is with the bow that we bring music to life and realize the composer's ideal. From the moment the bow touches the string it also characterizes the sound by the manner of its moving; therefore characterization and articulation are closely related both in technique and effect: you cannot characterize without articulation and you cannot articulate without conveying a certain character to the notes.

For articulation and phrasing, as well as an overall interpretative tool, bow technique relies basically on bow-speed, pressure, location and timing. While these essential elements are few, like the primary colours on the painter's palette, the infinite variety of their combinations is capable of expressing the music in every shade of its emotional, intellectual and artistic character. The following examples will demonstrate some of the possibilities.

Stressing the notes on the beat by slightly speeding-up the bow not only enhances the clarity of fast legato passages (provided the left-hand fingers are accurate) and ensures clean shifts on the beat, but also lends the needed crisp character and rhythmic vitality in:

Sonata No.3: first movement   *Beethoven*

Symphonie espagnole: first movement   *Lalo*

Similar means, but more delicate changes in bow-speed and pressure, combined with timing, add expressive and emotional intensity to:

Violin Concerto: Canzonetta   *Tchaikovsky*

To bring out the great difference one changed note makes in the otherwise identical phrases in the slow movement of the Brahms Concerto, delay and hold the top c'''' noticeably longer than its value (agogic accent) to indicate its greater emotional intensity than that of the corresponding *a'''* in the earlier phrase:

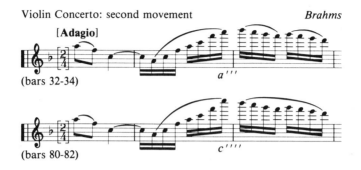

Violin Concerto: second movement   *Brahms*

(bars 32-34)

(bars 80-82)

The following phrase, on the other hand, needs to be precipitated with urgency toward the top of the phrase, which, marked by a *sf*, is then held slightly longer:

Violin Concerto: first movement   *Mendelssohn*

To realize the difference in effect, play these passages with a completely unvarying bow-stroke, even speed, steady pressure and identical tempo and dynamics (except for the '*sf*'): they will sound exceedingly dull and unmusical. Important as it is to be able to draw a perfectly even bow when circumstances demand, it is just as vital to be able to differentiate between notes and phrases and to treat them individually according to their musical prominence and character.

    Bow-speed is an essential characterizing factor both in starting and ending a stroke. Fast bow, or extra speed at the start indicates and accentuates energy and brilliance:

Preludium and Allegro   *Kreisler*

Slowing down the bow at the end of a note or stroke can give the impression of sadness or nostalgia:

Introduction and Rondo capriccioso   *Saint-Saëns*

The speed with which the bow touches the string in off-string, short-note passages—so frequent in string literature—is especially important: the bow must be in full speed to ensure the brightness, energy and carrying-power of the notes:

Violin Concerto No.4, K.218: last movement   *Mozart*

This is also one of the few bow-strokes where the right-hand fingers participate actively in moving the bow.

Bow-pressure, which usually increases as the bow-speed diminishes, should remain supple and effortless (remember the larger muscles!), and allow all the freedom of expression to your tone, which should be pulled out of the instrument, not squeezed in.

Generally speaking, when there is a choice, it is preferable to use more bow-speed and bow-amount than pressure, especially in passages of higher dynamic levels requiring greater carrying power, as this will increase the amplitude of the string vibrations. Keep in mind also that composers' slurs are usually phrasing marks and not bowings, which allow bow-changes during the same phrase, provided the phrasing remains clear and the change unnoticeable.

The location of the bow between the bridge and the fingerboard depends on the mixture of speed and pressure, the three being interdependent. It can also be the dominant factor when colour is the most important consideration, as in:

Poème   *Chausson*

Near the fingerboard, the bow also creates a light-textured, breezy character:

Sonata No.5 ('Spring'): opening   *Beethoven*

Closer to the bridge, as in the slow movement of the same sonata, with less speed and more pressure, the result is a more concentrated sound, better suited to the intimate and deeply felt character:

Sonata No.5 ('Spring'): second movement   *Beethoven*

You do not always have freedom of choice in the combination or proportion of these basic elements—quite often the circumstances dictate them. In this passage you have to use a very slow-moving bow fairly near the bridge and concentrated but elastic pressure, as the phrase does not allow any additional bow-change:

Violin Concerto: second movement   *Beethoven*

This type of bowing—important and frequently used—is well described by its French name: *son filé* = spun tone. Practise it regularly by playing long notes near the bridge with minimum speed and the maximum pressure that good tone-quality allows. At first the sound will be unpleasant, but by using the proper muscles and finding the right location (remember: the slower the bow, the greater the pressure, the closer to the bridge), you should eventually be able to draw a solid *f* sound for about 30 seconds—a very long time! When you do have the freedom to choose the bowing, as in this passage, take advantage of it and divide the slur indicated by the composer:

Violin Concerto: first movement — Beethoven

(original bowing)

Not only will it sound and carry better but, without changing its legato character, it will bring out the four 'g's to remind the listener of the four timpani strokes with which the concerto begins.

Since articulation and characterization are closely related, and since the character of a note or stroke is revealed the moment you put the bow to the string, the manner of starting and ending a stroke assumes great importance. In some instances technical necessities or musical considerations make a specific way of starting or ending obvious or unavoidable. More often than not, however, the choice will be up to you. Among the decisions you will have to make are:

(1)   whether to start a note from the string or from the air;
(2)   whether you want an accent or 'bite' at the beginning or not;
(3)   whether to end the note or stroke on or off the string;
(4)   whether to start the bow at full speed or not;
(5)   whether the tone should remain full or taper at the end.

In any case, your decision will depend on the character of the note, stroke or passage in question.

Here are some examples for various beginnings and endings. Starting from the string is appropriate for a sustained, lyric character and creates a clean, pure sound:

Adagio in E, K.261 — Mozart

but it can also express a dramatic, powerful beginning:

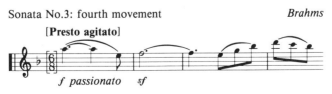

Sonata No.3: fourth movement — Brahms

[Presto agitato]

f passionato   sf

Up-bow starts, especially in the upper half, are usually from the string:

Violin Concerto: first movement　　　　　　　　　　　　　　*Mendelssohn*

In some works of virtuoso character, starting up-bow by slamming it on the string near the tip can be very effective, as in:

Violin Concerto: first movement　　　　　　　　　　　　*Paganini*

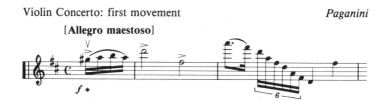

or for an accentuated up-bow chord:

Violin Concerto: third movement　　　　　　　　　　　　*Brahms*

Chords can be played either from the string or from the air, depending on style and tempo. A fast succession of chords has to be from the air:

Caprice No.1　　　　　　　　　　　　　　　　　　　*Dont*

but the chords in this fugue are from the string:

Sonata No.1: Fuga　　　　　　　　　　　　*Bach*

A very unusual case, involving four-note chords in *p* played from the string near the tip, very quickly and lightly broken, up-bow, is:

Sonata No.6: third movement, variation 4

Beethoven

Starting from the air often fits the character of short, energetic notes:

Sonata No.3: third movement

Beethoven

and also dramatic, impetuous, accentuated strokes:

Violin Concerto: third movement

Brahms

Fast spiccato passages are better started from the string as in:

Caprice No.5

Paganini

but, if using the original ricochet bowing, start from the air:

Caprice No.5

Paganini

Starts with a 'bite' usually mean extra speed and pressure:

Violin Concerto No.2: first movement   *Vieuxtemps*

f attacca con molto forza

A related melodic shape, but with a different character and an unaccentuated start is:

Sonata No.3: first movement   *Brahms*

p sotto voce ma espressivo

The manner of ending a note or stroke is equally characteristic and should not be left to chance. Stopping the bow on the string at the end of a note or passage creates a neat, crisp, but clipped and dry sound, whereas lifting the bow off the string permits the vibrations to continue and gives a free, ringing tone. (This effect is the same as when using the sustaining pedal on the piano, which lifts the dampers off the strings.) It is especially appropriate when the note or stroke is followed by a rest:

Violin Concerto No.3, K.216: first movement

Mozart

Otherwise, its effect can become unmusical:

Since lifting and replacing the bow in the upper half is impractical, the two different stroke endings should be combined within the same phrase, as in the following example:

Adagio in E, K.261   *Mozart*

on the string   off the string

Full bow-speed at the start is also used when there is an emphasis on each note:

Sonata: fourth movement   *Franck*

Whether to lift the bow off the string between notes of dotted rhythms is a frequent dilemma for which the answer lies in the character and tempo of the music. Off-string is better here, expecially since there is a rest indicated between the two notes:

Sonata No.1: first movement   *Brahms*

and, though there is no rest, even in:

Violin Concerto: first movement   *Mendelssohn*

On-string is better in:

Rondo brillant   *Schubert*

and in faster tempi (upper half):

The Art of Bowing: variation 8   *Tartini*

Sonata No.9 ('Kreutzer'): third movement   *Beethoven*

Phrase endings usually mean slowing down the bow on the string but this does not necessarily indicate sadness or resignation:

The end of the down-bow in the following example must, by contrast, finish with the bow in full speed to indicate its energy and brilliance and to point to the next note. The bow is then taken off the string, still in full speed, and returned in the air to near the frog for the next up-bow note:

BOWINGS AND EXPRESSION

The Basic Bowings and their Variants

(1) Détaché (Fr.):
(No It. used)

Single strokes, one note per bow, sustained and connected with no breaks or stops between notes. This is often translated incorrectly as 'detached', *ie* disconnected.

Variants:
Porté (Fr.) or
Portato (It.):

Emphasis, or added inflection at the beginning of each détaché stroke.

Collé (Fr.)
(No It. used):

The long version of this bowing variant, basically an off-string détaché: the bow is slightly lifted between long notes; used in lower half.

(2) Legato (It.):
(No Fr. used)

Two or more notes on the same bow, tied or slurred uninterrupted. Often incorrectly translated to mean merely 'smooth'.

Variant:
Louré (Fr.):
(sometimes also
Portato, It.)

A slightly articulated, pulsating legato.

(3) Martelé (Fr.)
Martellato (It.):

Short, single strokes, one note per bow, with stops between strokes. The bow usually moves rapidly and remains on string during the stops.

Variants:
Lancé (Fr.):
(No It. used)

Somewhat longer martelé (or somewhat shorter détaché), the bow faster at the beginning.

Collé (Fr.):
(No It. used)

Off-string martelé: short single notes pinched from the string, the bow off-string between notes.

Fouetté, or
Jeté (Fr.):

A short single note attacked from the air ('whipped', 'thrown' or 'slapped'), usually mixed with legato strokes, up-bow.

(4) Staccato (It.):
(No Fr. used)

A series of short notes, two or more per bow, separated by short stops, the bow remaining on string. (A series of martelé notes on the same bow in the same direction.)

Variant:
Staccato Volante (It.) or
Staccato Volant (Fr.):

Similar to staccato, except bow is off-string between notes: 'flying staccato'.

(5) Spiccato (It.) or
Sautillé (Fr.):

Bouncing bow; short, single strokes, one note per bow, off-string between notes.

Variant:
'On-string' Spiccato (Eng.)
(No Fr. or It.)

High-speed spiccato with no time between the notes to bounce off-string. The hair remains mostly on-string, and the bow-stick oscillates slightly up and down.

(6) Saltato or Saltando (It.) or
Ricochet (Fr.):

Rebounding bow: two or more notes per bow, the bow rebounds between each note during the same bow as a result of the initial attack.

Since different bowings are often marked in the same way, the player must decide which specific ones to use on each occasion.

This chart gives the definition of the various bowings, but within these definitions there is a wide range of character and expression.

The six basic bowings can be grouped into three pairs according to their musical characteristics:

Détaché }
Legato } on-string, sound sustained for full time-value

Martelé }
Staccato } on-string short notes, sound only half of time-value

Spiccato }
Ricochet } off-string short notes, sound only half of time-value

The first pair of bowings produces legato sounds, and the second and third pairs represent four ways of creating staccato sounds on stringed instruments.

―――――――――――

Détaché is the most basic bowing, since every time we change the bow, we are in fact using the détaché stroke. For that reason it is also the primary means of articulation and phrasing. It is 'detached' only in the sense that the separate successive notes in a passage, although sustained, are not slurred—one note per bow. Within this definition the détaché stroke can assume a variety of characters, from the smooth, unaccentuated:

to the brilliant, energetic and accentuated (but still sustained):

and the 'gypsy' stroke sometimes called 'parlando', a mixture of détaché and martelé:

By accentuating the low notes, you can bring out the built-in accompaniment in this passage:

Partita No.3: Preludium   *Bach*

You can also create the illusion of spiccato without the bow leaving the string in very fast passages ('on-string spiccato') when the rapid succession of notes leaves no time for the bow to bounce:

Moto Perpetuo   *Paganini*

Suggestions for Practice

Practise this variant of the détaché (or spiccato) stroke by using an extremely small amount of bow and considerable pressure in the middle of the bow, holding your right elbow slightly higher than normal.

For good tone quality in détaché use at least a minimum amount of pressure on every note, but especially on the up-bow, which is constitutionally weaker; using merely the weight of the bow for pressure gives a whistling, shallow sound.

Legato marks by most composers indicate phrasings, not bowings, and the player may change the bow several times within the same phrase, provided the bow-change is unnoticeable. An uninterrupted, seamless bow-change and a succession of perfectly even-toned strokes, creating the impression of an endless bow, are perhaps the most important and difficult goals of string playing, and the hallmark of a great player. They characterized the great artists of the past and were the result of long hours of slow open-string practice. In this long and very slow passage you obviously have to change the bow several times, but give the impression of an uninterrupted melodic line with no audible bow-change:

Sonata No.10: second movement   *Beethoven*

(Beethoven's phrasing)   *p*   *dim.*

In the following phrase, on the other hand, differentiation in speed and pressure while maintaining the legato character will gently stress the ♩s, giving a flowing, yet rhythmical and jovial expression:

Sonata No.6: third movement   *Beethoven*

This bowing ![portato marks] is a gentler version of the louré, or portato, a variant of legato, which is a basic, essential means of expressive bow technique. More dramatic characterization, using a sharper stress and greater bow-speed, will create greater tension and express the ominous character hinted at by the distant thunder-like rumblings of the piano bass in:

Sonata No.7: first movement   *Beethoven*

Rhythmical precision and evenness in fast legato passages depends largely on the left-hand fingers, but the bow also plays a substantial part in them. It can help the evenness of notes by allocating equal amounts of bow to each note, with special regard for string-crossings:

Violin Concerto: third movement   *Beethoven*

It can also stress the notes on each beat by increased bow-speed and pressure, to give these runs a rhythmical underpinning and clarity of articulation:

Sonata: second movement   *Franck*

Shifting on the beat, whenever possible, also helps clarity of articulation by the left hand.

In long, fast legato runs which are not differentiated rhythmically by the composer, it is very helpful to subdivide the passage into shorter rhythmic units and stress them by the bow (during practice) and mentally (during the performance). Much greater clarity and rhythmical precision can be achieved this way:

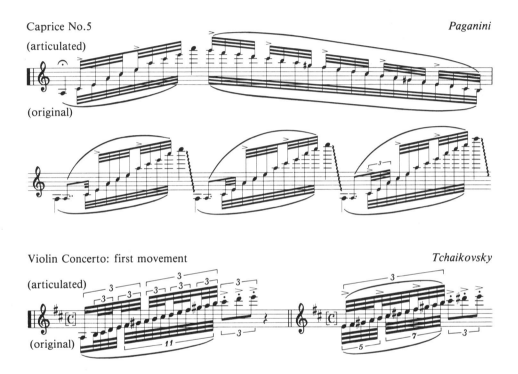

The second and third pairs of bowings consist of short notes: martelé and spiccato are single-note strokes, while staccato and ricochet have several notes on one stroke.

The choice between martelé and spiccato for a specific passage depends again on character, but also to a great extent on tempo. The martelé stroke has its own speed limit due to the alternation of pressure and release between the notes. The spiccato stroke, besides having no limit in speed or tempo, also has a totally different character. In contrast to the dry, clipped quality of the martelé, created by the bow's abrupt stopping on the string, the spiccato, by taking off between the notes, allows the string to vibrate in a continuing resonance and produces a free, ringing tone. The martelé stroke, in line with its technique and character, indicates a certain tension, while the spiccato, where the elasticity of the bow does half the work, gives a feeling of ease and lightness.

Some violinists seem to have difficulty with spiccato bowing. Yet it has much in common with the détaché, especially if the elasticity of the bow is allowed to do part of the job. The main difference in bow technique between détaché and spiccato is that the bow-arm section which moves the bow at a given speed does not move parallel with the bow as in the détaché, but is slightly more vertically slanted. The greater force with which the bow hits the string causes it to rebound, ready to drop again for the next note. Observe the following:

(1)   The right elbow should be held somewhat higher than normal; the spiccato should be thought of as a bowing in which the bow drops *down* and bounces back to a higher platform and not one in which the initial effort is to jump *up*. The bow-hold should be light to preserve elasticity. The motion of the forearm or hand (depending on tempo) is very similar to bouncing a rubber ball in front of you on an imaginary surface at the level of your waist.

(2)   As in the détaché, be sure to use the appropriate arm-section and the proper part of the bow for every speed and tempo: for a very fast spiccato use the hand around the middle of the bow or slightly above (depending on the properties of each particular bow); as the tempo slows down, use more and more the forearm and the lower part of the bow; for a slow spiccato use the whole arm, which now follows the same path as the bow for each individual note.

(3)   As the tempo gets slower, the *sound value* of the note remains *short*— it is the *rest* which gets *longer* and longer, therefore keep the bow, after leaving the string, moving in the air until it is time for the next note.

(4)   Make sure that the left-hand finger-actions and string-crossings are co-ordinated with the bow-strokes: very often the difficulties with spiccato arise from failure to do so. Practise spiccato passages as détaché at first, then the string-crossing patterns on open strings, and only after that as spiccato. Here are some examples from Paganini's 5th Caprice:

(1)   detaché, very little bow:

(2)   open strings, détaché, very little bow:

(3) spiccato:

The martelé stroke is indicated by the character of the following examples:

Sonata No.7: first movement   *Beethoven*

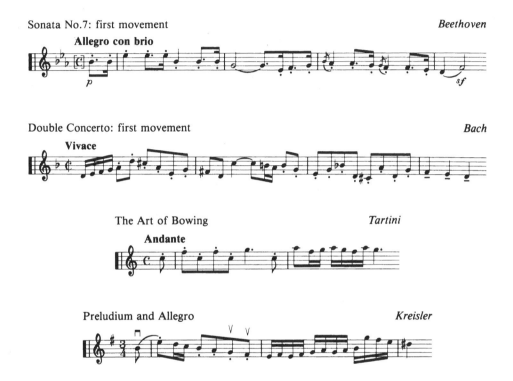

Double Concerto: first movement   *Bach*

The Art of Bowing   *Tartini*

Preludium and Allegro   *Kreisler*

while off-string bowing is more suitable for these:

Sonata No.10: third movement   *Beethoven*

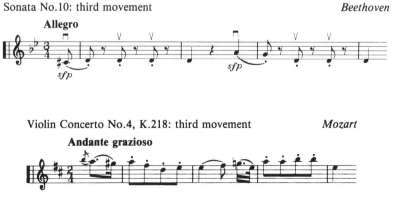

Violin Concerto No.4, K.218: third movement   *Mozart*

This type of bowing is no longer called spiccato, a term which implies a certain minimum speed; it is used often for longer, off-string notes of various expressive qualities:

Sonata No.3: third movement   *Brahms*

Note that a slur over several staccato notes usually lengthens their sound value.

Placing the bow on the string, without any noise, at all points along its length requires great bow control. The following exercise will be very useful in acquiring or improving it. Lift the bow between each note:

No.2 (42 Studies)   *Kreutzer*

There is also a bowing combination which might be called 'off-string martelé'. In this stroke, usually in moderate tempo, the bow is lifted off the string at the end of each note, but replaced immediately on the string, starting the next note again from the string. It is very useful for preserving the precision of the martelé without its customary dryness, as in this example:

Partita No.3: Gavotte   *Bach*

The very fast staccato and ricochet bowings are used mostly for special virtuoso effects, which does not exclude their choice for musical reasons also:

Violin Concerto: first movement   *Wieniawski*

Violin Concerto: first movement

Mendelssohn

ricochet

The Art of Bowing: variation 6

Tartini

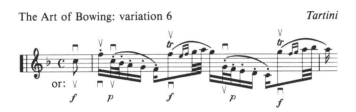

Although a very fast staccato stroke is largely a matter of innate ability (and is usually paired with a fast vibrato), it can be learned and improved with practice. There are several ways of doing this stroke:

(1)   As a tremolo near the tip, in which every other note is left out; in the up-bow staccato, which is by far the more often used version, leave out all the down-bows, which will result in an up-bow motion; for a down-bow staccato, leave out all the up-bows;

(2)   By rapidly alternating extra pressure and release while moving the bow up or down, (several one-directional martelé strokes)

(3)   By a very fast, trill-like action between the right-hand fingers and thumb, interrupting momentarily the movement of the bow, and

(4)   By slightly stiffening the bow-arm into a benign cramp.

You have to experiment before deciding which of these motions you can do most rapidly. If you choose the last method, be careful not to over-practise as your arm muscles may get hurt.

As in spiccato, the rapid staccato stroke has to be precisely co-ordinated with the left-hand finger-actions and string-crossings; quite often this bowing is unsuccessful because these conditions are not met.

In moderate tempi, both the on-string and off-string staccato bowings (in effect, a series of up-bow détaché, or spiccato notes) are very useful in equalizing uneven bow-distribution:

Sonata No.7: third movement, Trio

Beethoven

Without them you would eventually 'run out' of bow, as the down-bows are longer than the separate strokes. In many instances, however, when these bowings cannot be used for technical or musical reasons, you have to make up the lost bow-amounts by other means. In the following passage on the string use proportionately more bow on the up-bows (but without making them louder or longer). This will get you back to the point of departure:

Brandenburg Concerto No.3: first movement   *Bach*

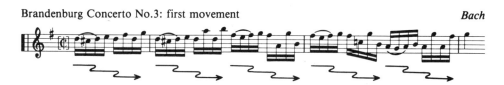

while in this passage off the string the longer down-bow can be equalized by continuing the up-bow in the air for an equal distance:

Double Concerto: third movement   *Brahms*

The very fast version of the off-string staccato is called the 'flying staccato':

Zapateado   *Sarasate*

In passages where short, off-string strokes are mixed with longer, on-string ones, it is much better to play the on-string stroke down-bow in the middle of the bow or in the lower half, which will avoid a shaky landing on the string:

Violin Concerto: third movement   *Mendelssohn*

Watch out for giving a wrong accent on a light beat; accentuate the preceding heavy beat—unless, of course, the composer wants it the other way, as in:

Sonata No.1: third movement   *Beethoven*

Whatever bowing you decide to use, the most frequent decision in phrasing will be whether to play a note or passage up-bow or down-bow. This is not just a technical choice, since the logic of musical language demands that:

(1) up-beats and light beats should be up-bow
(2) down-beats and heavy beats should be down-bow
(3) loud notes or passages use the lower half of the bow
(4) soft notes or passages use the upper half of the bow.

In practice, however, logic does not always produce a musical result and you should learn to look for alternative solutions. These often become apparent only when you practise the whole phrase and find out where, if anywhere, there *must* be an up-bow or down-bow, due to musical or technical reasons. In the following phrase, beginning with a very light beat (in effect an upbeat to the second heaviest beat in the ₵ measure), logic would dictate that you start up-bow and duly arrive down-bow on the heavy down-beat at the beginning of the next bar. Playing on, and following Beethoven's phrasing mark of two slurred notes, however, you will discover that the down-beat of the third bar will be up-bow, which is not only too light for the down beat, but following the spiccato notes, very awkward to manage. The solution is to back-track to the beginning of the phrase, start down-bow near the tip to keep the up-beat light, use enough bow to get to the middle for the spiccato passage and also provide the stress for the heavy down-beat in up-bow, and finish the phrase down-bow on the heavy beat of the third bar, which must be down-bow:

Sonata No.5 ('Spring'): fourth movement   *Beethoven*

Sometimes, having chosen a seemingly correct bow direction for a succession of phrases, you may discover that to follow it to its logical conclusion would either lead you to the wrong heavy-beat—light-beat distribution, or disturb the mood of the music. The beginning of this phrase would logically be an up-bow, but this would lead either to an up-bow on the heavy down-beat of bar 9, which must be down-bow, or it would necessitate a quick back-take of the bow in bar 7, upsetting the calm serenity of the moment. It is better to start with a weightless down-bow and of a light up-beat quality, stressing slightly the up-bow down-beat, and arrive down-bow in bar 9 and following bars:

Sonata: first movement, opening   *Franck*

In the following example, on the other hand, the two successive upbows, restoring the down-up succession, are well in character with the piece and the martelé strokes. (Try the up-bow start: it is much less natural.) Take care, however, to give a strong accent on the first down-beat to counteract the down-bow, up-beat beginning:

Preludium and Allegro   *Kreisler*

Since you cannot always have the availability of a down-bow for a down-beat or the up-bow for the up-beat, you should be able to indicate a heavy beat up-bow and to play a light beat down-bow. In deciding whether to use an up-bow or down-bow, you must also consider which part of the bow to use. You should also know in advance, for the sake of equal bow-distribution, how much bow you will need. In the following similar phrases:

(1)   Start the up-bow slightly below the middle, so that you have the whole bow for the following down-bow:

Sonata No.1: third movement   *Brahms*

(2)   Later in the movement, it is better to play the 2nd and 3rd dotted rhythms with separate bows in order to have the whole bow for the next, longer phrase, first at the tip, then at the frog:

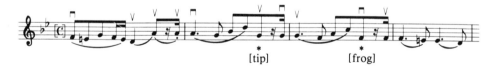

The various sections of the bow also have musical characteristics. The lower half and vicinity of the frog can give strength, effortless power and projection even in fast legato passages; the upper half is more suitable for lightness and agility. Ideally, even when circumstances deny the choice, the player should be able to express, or give the impression of, any musical character and mood at any part of the bow.

Occasionally, faster strokes can also be played at the frog or in the lower half, in which case the upper arm also participates in the motion. This has the advantage of easy pressure from the weight of the arm. Agility at that point can be acquired by practising fast détaché études and string-crossings at the frog. The time devoted to this phase of bow technique will be well spent.

Bow-section, amount and location can also be combined for various character and colouristic effects. An imaginative and contrasting combination of this is:

Caprice No.9   *Paganini*

while playing the following passage near the bridge (sul ponticello), lends it a distorted, nightmarish character:

Tzigane   *Ravel*

Whatever your technical decisions, they should always be based on musical grounds and knowing what are the musical effects that the various technical means can accomplish. Try to have a fully developed, ideal conception of the whole work. Look beyond the notes into the music and its meaning before you decide on the most natural and fitting technical solution.

8 PHRASING AND INTERPRETATION I

Speech is the audible version of language. In speaking, we can express not only the precise sound equivalent of the written text, but, by various shadings, accents and pacings of the voice, we can convey its deeper meaning.

Musical performance is very similar. Written musical symbols should be transformed from the visual into the audible medium not only within their narrow, literal limits, but with all the expressive qualities inherent in the music. In putting musical ideas on paper, the composer is hampered by an inadequate system of notation, which is capable of indicating only the primary features of music. Even so, the essence of music cannot be wholly expressed and notated on paper ('music begins where words fail'): there is much more to music than merely following the written symbols, no matter how accurately.

The performer, therefore, has more freedom, but also the greater responsibility, of contributing a personal insight and understanding to the music, while still respecting the composer's specific instructions and preserving his style. In this dual obligation the player must not only follow the written indications, but also discover and express the deeper meaning and emotional content of the music. The music is not only translated from the visual to the audible; it is a language that needs an interpreter.

The clues towards this deeper understanding are found among such unwritten notions as the interaction of keys and harmonies, modulation, the shape of a melodic line, and the form of a piece. To interpret the clues you will have to 'read between' the (bar) lines. Your sensitivity to these subtle details and individual solutions to the clues will put a personal stamp on the music.

In addition to a thorough knowledge of a composer's language, it is also often necessary to know about the composer's personality and his times. Robert Schumann, in a letter to his future wife, the pianist Clara Wieck, explains this well:

> I am affected by everything that goes on in the world, and think it over in my own way, politics, literature and people, and then I long to express my feelings and find an outlet for them in music. That is why my compositions are sometimes difficult to understand, because they are connected with distant interests, and sometimes striking, because everything extraordinary that happens impresses me and compels me to express it in music.
>
> *Letters of Composers*
> (Alfred A. Knopf, New York, 1907)

When you read a book or a newspaper, you 'hear' it and understand the text within your brain, pronouncing it silently. In the same way, when you read a musical text, you should instantly hear it in your inner ear as it is supposed to sound, whether you have absolute or relative pitch. For this reason, the importance of early and thorough training in sol-fa and solfège, sightsinging, ear-training, harmony and theory cannot be emphasized strongly enough.

Since in string playing it is the bow which conveys most of the expression and deeper meaning of music, and since the greatest bow technique is of little use without something to express, you should have a very clear idea of what the music you are playing wants to express, what your own interpretation of it is, and how it is to be performed in terms of bow technique. The possibility of different, yet valid interpretations of the same piece stems partly from the nature of music, partly from the method of notating it, and partly from the different personalities performing it. The written word is a much more precise way of notating a language and comes much closer to its meaning, yet there is often more than one way to interpret many a written text, poem or play.

Interpretation can also be seen as composition in reverse; starting from the finished work and retracing the composer's path to the original idea, or as composing an opera backwards, adding a libretto after the music is finished. Providing a libretto can often be very helpful toward finding a way to interpret an instrumental piece. Try to invent a story or scenario for the mood and character of the piece, in which the high and low points coincide with those of the composition. Whether the composer had any story or scene in mind is immaterial. Your own invention might bring the music closer to you and, through you, to the audience.

Articulation, phrasing and interpretation are distinct in concept but closely related, and they overlap both in effect and in technical execution. The relation-ship between articulation and phrasing is similar to the relationship between phrasing and interpretation: clarity of detail leads to clarity of overall concept.

Phrasing in music originates from the human voice, the ideal of most instrumental compositions. It stems not only from the logic of the musical language, but also from the singer's natural need to breathe. In string playing also, a phrase must be permitted to 'breathe' by the appropriate bow techniques of timing, changes in dynamics, bow-speed and articulation. In addition, the high and low points of a phrase can only be indicated and made clear by the same bow techniques.

In the following example a slight crescendo to a''' and an unnoticeable bow change indicate that the first two bars form one phrase-unit; the slight diminuendo and barely perceptible hesitation at the end of the second bar mark the end of the first phrase-unit and separate it from the next one, which continues the same train of musical thought. At the same time the high and low points in the phrase—*a'''* and *a''*—become clear, and a slight delay after *a''* marks the beginning of a new idea:

Violin Concerto: first movement   *Beethoven*

A similar phrase returns later in the same movement as a reminiscence, the low register (and the G string) giving it a more introspective character. This time the third bar needs additional articulation to underline the more frequent harmony changes in the orchestral accompaniment (on each beat), which also justify a slightly slower tempo. While technically this is a matter of articulation, musically it is a question of interpretation:

The phrasing in this opening theme can be brought out by articulation without agogics or changes in tempo, and by changes in dynamics and bow-speed. It is sufficient to make clear that the first half of the theme consists of two one-bar units and a related, extended two-bar unit, which cross the bar-lines. This needs technically a very slight diminuendo on the ♩s and a very slight crescendo leading up to them. The differentiations must be minimal and the effect as natural as singing or breathing.

Sonata No.2: third movement   *Brahms*

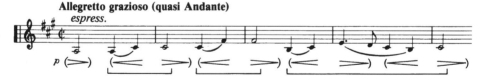

Similar articulation and bow technique can be used in this opening, a very slight slow-down of the bow (diminuendo) on the *f*, and a minimal increase in bow-speed (crescendo) on the ♪♪♪♪ passage leading up to it, without changing tempo:

Sonata No.5 ('Spring'): first movement   *Beethoven*

Sensitive bow-handling and articulation can bring out the happy, sunny character of the following theme, marked simply *p dolce*:

Sonata No.6: third movement   *Beethoven*

Remember, though, that these subtle stresses and accents added to Beethoven's markings should be barely perceptible.

The short note in legato dotted rhythm often suffers from one of two contrary flaws in performance: either it is neglected to the point of inaudibility, or separated from the long note, destroying the legato character and phrasing. In the following and similar examples the solution is to speed the bow very slightly for the short note, but without stopping or interrupting the bow:

Sonata No.3: Adagio   *Bach*

This is especially important when string-crossing or double-dotted rhythm is involved:

String Quartet Op.77, No.1: first movement   *Haydn*

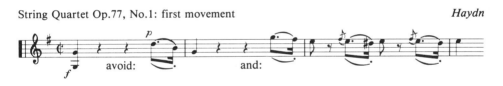

and

Sonata No.3: second movement   *Beethoven*

Sometimes the end of a phrase coincides with the beginning of the next and the phrases overlap:

Sonata No.1: Siciliano   *Bach*

If you bring out the end of the first phrase and assume that the *siciliano* motif begins with the ♪ note (as indeed it does in most instances in the movement) this is consistent with both the musical and technical demands. The first note at the beginning can be seen as merely establishing the tonality, and you can avoid breaking the chords downward—never a pleasant sound. In any case, in several places even that could not solve the problem because of the exigencies of the upper voices.

In another instance the first phrase is not yet finished when the next intrudes. Here a slight delay and a suddenly higher dynamic level can indicate the entrance of the precocious next phrase:

Chaconne   Bach

[*pochiss. rit. mf a tempo*]

The following, well-known, theme requires three different means of articulation, phrasing and expression, corresponding to its three, slightly different characters:

(1)   Solo violin, on the G string (Beethoven's marks), *p legato*.

Violin Concerto: third movement   *Beethoven*

(2)   Solo violin *p delicatamente* (Beethoven's marks), non-legato (staccato) as both the solo violin and the accompaniment are in a much higher register.

(3) Full orchestra tutti: *ff marcato.*

In deciding the way to phrase these examples, the rhythm of the accompaniment in (1) and (2) tells us a great deal. Two bars of whole-measure phrases are followed by one bar of two half-measure phrases and another whole-measure phrase. Technically this means that there should be only one accent in each of the first, second and fourth bars (on the down-beat), but two in the third bar. In (3), played *ff* by the whole orchestra, there is a striking change in character, and every beat requires an accent, *as well as* non-legato phrasing.

It is always important to know and listen to the accompaniment of the works you play (including the orchestral instrumentation, which is a great help in memorizing your entrances). If you know only the solo fraction of a work you cannot fully understand it.

9 PHRASING AND INTERPRETATION II

In music, not all notes are created equal. To a great extent their importance depends on their position and function in the music. The more prominent are emphasized by accents or stresses, which are either:

(1)   Explicit, indicated directly by the composer, or
(2)   Implied by their context.

From the point of view of their *technical execution*, there are also two distinct groups of accents:

(1)   *Dynamic accents*, which emphasize the note by a sudden increase in sound due to a momentary increase in bow-speed and/or pressure, and
(2)   *Agogic accents*, which stress a note by timing: by slightly delaying or lengthening it.

The agogic accent is more subtle than the dynamic accent and is rarely used by itself. The combination of the two can be most effective in the whole range of dynamics from *pp* to *ff*—the one reinforces the other and the impact depends on the ratio of the mixture. When the dynamic ingredient is minimal, the resulting mild accent can be called a stress, and is more suitable for implied accents, which should never be exaggerated. For maximum impact, combine a strong dynamic accent with the timing of an agogic accent: it will be power enough for the most dramatic, explicit, composer-indicated effect.

EXPLICIT ACCENTS

Indicated by the signs *sf, fz* or *sfz, fp*, *rinforzando* and **>**, or its more gradual version **< >**, explicit accents are generally stronger than implied accents, although their relative prominence is dictated by the context of the prevailing dynamic level and expressive intensity. *Subito f* also belongs to this group in effect, whereas *subito p* is an accent in reverse—a negative accent created by the sudden reduction of bow-speed and bow-pressure, usually preceded by a very slight pause. (The mark *pf* is often misinterpreted as *piano-forte*; in fact it means *poco forte*, and, to my knowledge, is used only by Brahms.)

The following examples illustrate various composer-indicated accents (note that *sf*, *sfz* and *fz* are used interchangeably, depending on the individual composer):

Dynamic accents:

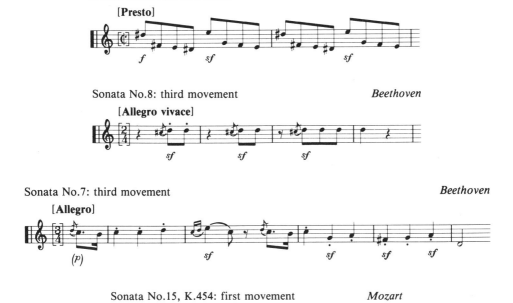

The extent, impact and corresponding bow technique depends on the context in which the accents are used: *sf* within a *f* dynamic range has to be stronger than in *p*, and the increase in bow-speed and pressure greater:

compared to later in the same movement:

87

Combined dynamic and agogic accents

These are appropriate for greater impact or expressive quality:

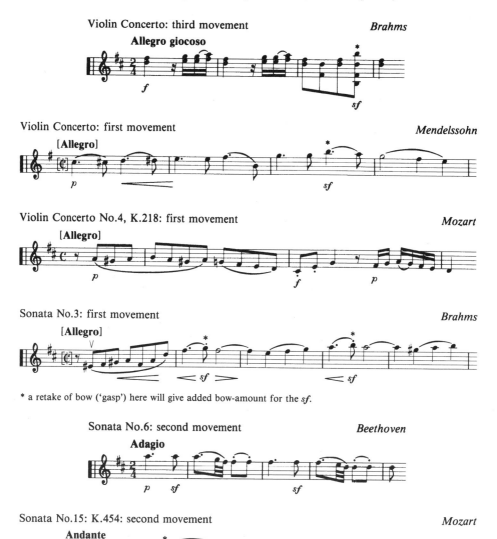

* a retake of bow ('gasp') here will give added bow-amount for the *sf*.

In the following example, the *p* (*subito*) is a sort of 'negative' accent:

IMPLICIT ACCENTS

Notes which have added importance due to their more prominent placement, function or character in the music, but which are not specifically marked by the composer, should be stressed sensitively by more subtle and discreet accents. Besides its strategic placement within the measure or group of measures, the prominence of a note can stem from its pivotal position in a melodic line or phrase, its role in a harmony, its derivation from trills or chords, or from rhythmic tension. Since the accents due to these notes are not specifically marked, it will be a personal decision—*interpretation*—as to when and how strongly these notes should be stressed.

While generally more subtle and less pronounced than explicit accents, their presence should be felt:

> ... accents, which are inherent in the shape the music takes, and which are present whether or not they demand special stress in performance, must, if the musical expression is to be clear, be underlined by *all* of the elements in the music, working, as it were, in co-ordination with each other ... Remember that *accent means contrast and vice versa.*
>
> Roger Sessions, *Harmonic Practice*
> (Harcourt Brace Jovanovich Inc., New York, 1951)

Technically, the agogic element should predominate in the performance of these accents to prevent their exaggeration. Sometimes it is even sufficient merely to *think* of a note—or of a rest, if it occurs on a heavy beat—as more prominent in order to ensure the clarity of a phrase.

Placement in the Measure or Group of Measures

An important clue here may be found in the composer's choice of time-signature. This gives a strong hint as to his musical thinking and should help in interpretation. The tradition of 'heavy' and 'light' beats in the various time-signatures which has developed in Western Classical music in the past 300 years places relatively more stress on the notes which fall on 'strong' beats. The evidence of this can be demonstrated by moving the bar-lines or changing the metre in a well-known melody. This simple device alters the importance of various notes, changes the harmonic structure, modifies the shape and phrasing of the melody and transforms its whole character. Consequently, the technical execution and accentuation need to be adjusted.

Now play the original:

Symphony No.4: second movement   *Tchaikovsky*

Notice in the following examples the difference between the time-signatures $\frac{3}{4}$ and $\frac{6}{8}$, $\frac{3}{2}$ and $\frac{6}{4}$, or $\frac{3}{8}$ and $\frac{6}{16}$: in each case, the first indicates three-beat bars, the second two or six, depending on tempo, but never three-beat bars. In the following the articulation makes the inherent accentuation clear:

Sonata No.1: last movement   *Bach*

and not:

However, differentiation between heavy and light beats does not mean that every note on a heavy beat should have a stress or an accent. Such playing gives the performance a repetitious, mechanical character. Just being aware of the difference will help to find the correct phrasing, whether it is across the bar or not, and will produce the most suitable bowing.

The following are two of the many instances when the bar-lines should be ignored. Within the $\frac{3}{4}$ time signature, Brahms hides a $\frac{3}{2}$ and $\frac{5}{4}$ metre respectively:

Violin Concerto: first movement   *Brahms*

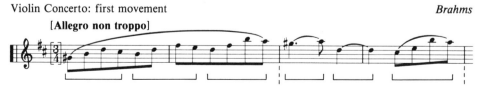

ibid: first movement

Changing the bar-lines and altering the note-values within the bar of the same sequence of notes can produce a metamorphosis:

Violin Concerto Op.61: first movement *Beethoven*

leading to:

Quartet in F Op.59, No.1: first movement *Beethoven*

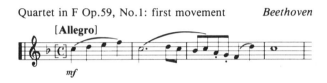

(The close opus numbers may explain such a relationship even if the composer—as is likely—was unaware of it.)

Phrasing may sometimes be obscured by ambiguous indications. In the following example the unexpected dynamic changes, as well as the changes of time-signature, tend to imply that the $\frac{2}{4}$ bars are the beginnings of three-measure phrases and the isolated $\frac{6}{8}$ bars are inserts, but a closer look may reveal a four-bar, common harmonic progression starting from these interpolations:

Sonata No.9 ('Kreutzer'): third movement

Beethoven

in E: V_7 VI   IV I_6

Seen like this in four-bar phrases, the f $\frac{6}{8}$ bars preceding the $\frac{2}{4}$ bars are the heavy measure and not the sudden $\frac{2}{4}$ p bars, which would be implied in a three-bar phrase. The relationship between 'heavy' and 'light' is the same in a three- or four-bar phrase as in a $\frac{3}{4}$ or $\frac{4}{4}$ measure.

Long, fast passages also sound clearer and more brilliant if the inherent accents are marked according to the melodic 'skeleton' and its 'poles of gravity':

Scherzo Tarantelle   *Wieniawski*

Pivotal position

In each of the following the high point of the melody implies a 'pivotal' change in phrasing:

Poème   *Chausson*

Violin Concerto: first movement   *Brahms*

Placement in the Harmonic Structure

Notes representing dissonances in the melody are endowed with added expressive importance and deserve agogic attention, as in the following examples.

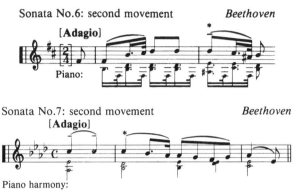

Thus, the long anticipated, yet unexpected resolution of the last seven bars in the third movement of the Franck Sonata becomes even more effective if the arrival of the F♯ minor chord is perceptibly delayed.

Trills

As a rule, trills imply an accent, although there are exceptions. Here, the trills emphasize the phrasing and need an accent:

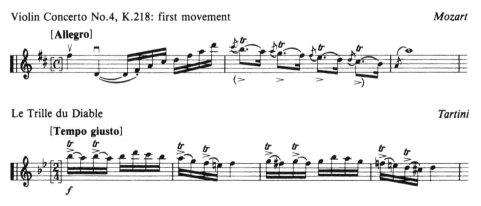

but these soft trills on a weak beat are without accent:

Chords

When a composer writes a chord on a string instrument, he is aware that technically it will acquire an accent as in:

Rhythmic Tension

Sometimes a composer links notes together in groupings which go across bar-lines *and* against the metre, implying a dynamic accent at the beginning of each group. In this case, as in most violinist-composers' works, bowing also implies phrasing:

Another example of bowing against the beat is the so-called 'Paganini' bowing:

'Moses' Fantasy   *Paganini*

Notes which are part of a hidden melody, theme or voice need to be brought out:

Partita No.3: Preludium   *Bach*

Hidden melody:

In an extreme case, the length of the agogic accents must be exaggerated for both musical and technical reasons where a succession of wide shifts, if played strictly in time, would create a slippery and unsettling effect:

Poème   *Chausson*

This should be modified approximately to:

Vibrato is also important in expressive, agogic accents (even though the left hand is outside the purview of this book): in effect, the vibrato in itself is a kind of expressive accent, and should complement the action of the bow.

Another class of implicit accents arises in music which has its origins in the dance. Dance forms such as the minuet and polonaise have their own inherent accentuation. The essence of dance is rhythm, and the essence of rhythm is accent.

Partita No.3: Menuet I   *Bach*

Polonaise in D
Wieniawski

Exceptions may be found among the slower dance forms, as well as in the following:

Violin Concerto No.5, K.219: Tempo di Menuetto
Mozart

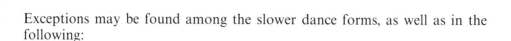

Syncopated notes, too, often imply accents. They are, and sound, in conflict with the on-beat pulse of the tempo. They may only be felt subconsciously, but are a driving force nevertheless and require reinforcement by accent.

Sonata No.3: fourth movement
Brahms

[**Presto agitato**]

Sonata No.2: third movement
Beethoven

[**Allegro piacevole**]

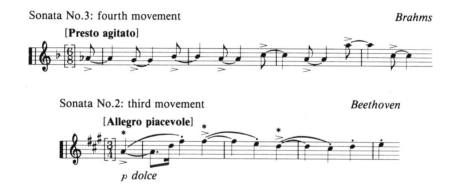

p dolce

Sometimes, an expressive version of syncopation needs a more gentle stress instead of an accent:

Sonata No.1: second movement
Brahms

[**Adagio**] *legato*

f espress.

Syncopated notes should not be confused with 'after-beats', where the first half of the beat consists of rest (silence): ♪ ♪ ♪ ♪ as opposed to: ♪♪♪♪. A very imaginative and original combination of syncopated notes and 'after-beats' serves as the accompaniment to the closing theme, shadowing and imitating its rhythm elsewhere in the same sonata:

Sonata No.1: first movement   *Brahms*

Rhythm and Tempo

The pre-eminence of rhythm in music has been established since the earliest times—in fact, in the beginning, rhythm *was* music. Its importance was reaffirmed at the dawn of the 'Classical' era by Leopold Mozart, among others, who wrote:

> Rhythm makes the melody, therefore rhythm is the soul of music; it not only animates the music but also maintains the orderly flow of its individual parts.
> *Treatise on the Fundamental Principles of Violin Playing*
> (Oxford University Press, New York, 1951)

This 'orderly flow' depends on, and is made possible by, the steady tempo-pulse mentioned, which is a most important factor in the rhythmical precision and clarity of any musical performance. We judge, measure and play the various rhythmical configurations, as well as the evenly paced notes, by superimposing them, consciously or subconsciously, on this silent, but ever-present background. As we may measure and learn to judge spatial distances with the help of a yardstick, which subdivides length and distances into smaller, equal units, so we may measure and gauge time—and rhythm—by *subdividing* the rhythmical figures in the mind into shorter, equal time-units:

Violin Concerto: third movement   *Brahms*

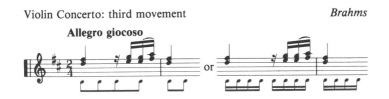

A useful yardstick of time is the metronome, with its ability to teach the equal subdivision of time, and to instil the feeling of a steady pulse. This is just as valuable as its function of telling speed and tempo. Practise and use it with this aspect in mind to develop rhythmic and motoric memory, to improve the sense of steady pulse and so sharpen the skill of subdividing time, without which there can be no rhythmical precision or vitality.

A successful performance and a convincing interpretation depend a great deal on choosing the 'right' tempo, one which makes the audience feel that it can be the 'only' one at that moment. This 'ideal' tempo of a piece may vary slightly from one player to another; it can change from time to time even for the same performer. Often the same tempo does not work for the whole piece: there need to be slight tempo changes, even without the composer's indication, to allow for the different moods and characters of the various themes.

To a degree, the style, character and category of the work, the personality of the player, the circumstances of the performance and the performance practices of the day will all have a certain influence on the choice of the tempo, which, however, should not digress far from the composer's indication. Taking that for a basis, a good rule to follow in deciding a slow tempo is that no matter how slow the tempo mark itself, there should always be forward momentum and direction, so that the notes can still be perceived as parts of a melodic line or progression, not as isolated sounds.

Conversely, no matter how fast the tempo, the music should not sound hurried or out of control. Phrases should 'breathe', rapid passages must be rhythmical and clearly articulated, and every note projected with full sound within the dynamic range. The performance should never appear laboured or give the impression that the tempo—or the piece—is beyond the player's technical capability. The fastest passage in the piece is often a good guide towards the right tempo, but, if still in doubt, try to find a section or phrase of which the tempo is self-evident: it will usually fit the rest of the work or movement.

The ability, dexterity and sensitivity to play the various accents in a musical, technically correct manner is an integral part of an advanced bow technique. Unmusical, wrong accents are caused not only by faulty bow technique, but also by misguided or careless musicianship... or simply by a failure to listen.

Nowhere is this more noticeable than in the concert hall, where everything is magnified. Just as an actor has to enunciate more clearly and speak with greater intensity in a theatre than in a small rehearsal room or in everyday conversation, the musician has to articulate more clearly, phrase more emphatically and with greater projection in the concert hall.

Since you cannot, and should not, change your technique every time you are confronted with different acoustics, most of the transformation from practice studio to concert platform can be achieved by the various devices of bow technique described in this book. Nevertheless, the ultimate shape of a performance will emerge only during the concert itself—the only phase of your art which you cannot practise at home.

10 CHECK-LIST III

(1)   Learn to listen to yourself and to hear yourself objectively.

(2)   Observe the relationship between heavy and light beats in your choice of bowings whenever possible, but maintain their character both in up- and down-bow.

(3)   Keep a balance between heavy and light beats: avoid monotonous accents on heavy beats (especially in down-bows and chords) and too weak up-bows in light or up-beats.

(4)   Adjust bow-speed, pressure and location in proportion to bow-amount; equalize uneven bow-distribution for proper phrasing.

(5)   Avoid sudden, unjustified changes in bow-speed which might cause musical and technical problems.

(6)   Choose bowings from a musical point of view, sometimes by back-tracking from a clearly imperative bowing.

(7)   In string-crossing, prepare and anticipate the bow action for an unnoticeable bow- and string change; accentuate or articulate for musical reasons only.

(8) Use bowings which are technically, musically and stylistically appropriate for the composition; match their character to that of the music.

(9) Be aware of the overall musical structure, the phrasing and the placement of notes and phrases within bar-lines and bar-groups.

(10) Practise and perfect your technique of articulation and phrasing; practise the *musical expression* most of all!

PROBLEM SOLVER'S INDEX